D0054128

DATE DUE

AP 25 '01			
OC 25 '01			
MR 14 '02			
MR 24 '03			
MR 20 03			
AP 10 03			
NO 4 '03			

Also by Ralph Keyes

. . . . .

We, the Lonely People
Is There Life After High School?
The Height of Your Life
Chancing It
Timelock
Sons on Fathers
"Nice Guys Finish Seventh"

The

COURAGE
TO WRITE

· · · · · · · · · · · · · · · ·

_How Writers
Transcend Fear_

RALPH KEYES

HENRY HOLT AND COMPANY · NEW YORK

Publishers since 1866
115 West 18th Street
New York, New York 10011

Henry Holt® is a registered
trademark of Henry Holt and Company, Inc.

Library of Congress Cataloging-in-Publication Data
Keyes, Ralph.
The courage to write: how writers transcend fear
/ Ralph Keyes—1st ed.
p.   cm.
Includes bibliographical references.
1. Authorship—Psychological aspects.   2. Authors—Psychology.
3. Creation (Literary, artistic, etc.).   4. Emotions.   I. Title.
PN171.P83K49   1995   94-39800
808'.02'019—dc20   CIP

ISBN 0-8050-3188-X

Henry Holt books are available for special
promotions and premiums. For details contact:
Director, Special Markets.

First Edition—1995

Designed by Victoria Hartman

Printed in the United States of America
All first editions are printed on acid-free paper. ∞

10   9   8   7   6   5   4   3

For my brother Steve,
who has courage

Contents

II · Coming to Terms with Fear

Acknowledgments

I would like to acknowledge help from the following people: Judith Appelbaum, Bill Baker, Imogene Bolls, Richard Bullock, Gay Courter, Philomène d'Ursin, Richard Farson, Dan Friedman, Jonellen Heckler, Robert Inman, Maura Jacoby, Arno Karlen, Layne Longfellow, Musa Mayer, Ruth Myers, and Kathryn Olney.

Librarians at the Yellow Springs public library and Antioch College library—Jan Miller especially—were unusually helpful.

My editor, Theresa Burns, gave me fine support and helpful comments. My agent, Colleen Mohyde, devoted more time to this project than a client should reasonably expect, and the book's a better one for it. My children, David and Scott, took an active interest in its progress. As always, my wife, Muriel, was my best source of support, help, and shrewd manuscript assessment.

I would also like to express my appreciation to the following authors and publications for granting me permission to use previously printed material: "Shadow of a Man" by Randy Alexis (*New York Day by Day: Poetry of the Homeless* by David Bird and Sarah Rimer), copyright ©

I

The Elements of Courage

. . . .

Writing as an Act of Courage

*If we had to say what writing is,
we would have to define it essentially
as an act of courage.*
—*Cynthia Ozick*

E. B. White was the most graceful of writers. A generation of imitators tried, but seldom succeeded, to match his casual self-assurance. We like to imagine White on his New England farm dashing off lighthearted essays and charming books for children when he wasn't slopping hogs or chopping wood. In fact, White worried over every word. He rewrote pieces twenty times or more and sometimes pleaded with the postmaster of North Brooklin, Maine, to return a just-mailed manuscript so he could punch up its ending or rewrite the lead.

In addition to being a consummate rewriter, White was a gifted procrastinator. By writing long letters and puttering about his farm, he often managed to avoid the trauma of writing altogether. When the *Paris Review* wanted to interview him for its *Writers at Work* series, White said he'd be better qualified for one on *Writers* Not *at Work*. White later told his friend James Thurber that he considered himself "the second most inactive writer living, and the third most discouraged."

This would have surprised readers of his essays. To them, E. B. White was a courageous interpreter of the world's vagaries. That wasn't how he saw himself. After the president of Dartmouth College paid tribute to his "literary bravery," White thought, "He little knew." Dartmouth's president made that remark while conferring an honorary degree on the nation's favorite essayist. This was a rare occasion in which White had been lured from his farm onto a public platform. As he sat there, White later wrote his wife, "the old emptiness and dizziness and vapors seized hold of me. . . . Nobody who has never suffered my peculiar kind of disability can understand the sheer hell of such moments."

Elwyn Brooks White had a lifelong fear of making public appearances. In his elementary school, students were called on to recite in alphabetical order of their last names. White spent long, agonizing hours dreading his fate as classmates whose names began with the alphabet's first twenty-two letters strode to the front of the room. Recitation wasn't his only childhood fear. Other things that scared White included darkness, girls, lavatories, the future, and the "fear that I was unknowing about things I should know about." Although he outgrew some of these anxieties, others took their place. White's fear of school bathrooms was replaced by concern that the brakes would fail on a trolley taking him up or down a hill. When he no longer needed to fret about reciting in class, White worried about collapsing on the street. By adding and subtracting fears this way, he kept himself in a steady state of anxiety. "Much of the story of the life of E. B. White," wrote biographer Scott Elledge, "is the story of how he has come to terms with his fears."

The most effective strategy of all was to turn them into stories. White's books for children conveyed a tone of apprehension with the sure voice of an expert. Stuart Little found Manhattan no less frightening than his creator did. Wilbur the pig, in *Charlotte's Web*, was as scared of dying as his literary parent (though with more justification). The best of White's work had an edgy flavor that *demanded* readers pay attention. Joseph Epstein has pointed out the many anxious, almost macabre elements in White's deceptively "light" essays: a henhouse consumed with "contagious hysteria and fear"; "faces desperate in the rain"; "the fierce bewildering night." One of E. B. White's best essays—"The Second Tree from the Corner"—describes a Whitelike man named Trexler who consults a psychiatrist about his crippling anxieties. Unable to answer the psychiatrist's questions, Trexler nonetheless leaves his office feeling unburdened, "unembarrassed at being afraid; and in the jungle of his fear he glimpsed (as he had so often glimpsed them before) the flashy tail feathers of the bird courage."

White personified courage by being so willing to sail boldly into the squall of his own fears, commenting on the trip as he went. That's why we took to him. This man seemed at least as anxious as we were, but more willing to own up to it. "I am not inclined to apologize for my anxieties," he once said, "because I have lived with them long enough to respect them." When it came to his calling, White wrote eloquently about how much courage it took to write. "A writer's courage can easily fail him," he observed while accepting the National Medal for Literature. "I feel this daily."

In his simplest testament of all, White said, "I admire anybody who has the guts to write anything at all."

A Dangerous Career

The saga of E. B. White tells us something about writing fears and the courage to write. On the one hand, anxiety is inevitable among those who put words on paper for others to read. On the other hand, fear can be transcended, can even be made part of the writing process itself. Doing this takes courage. Few authors would dispute that. In talking with writers on this subject and reading about them, I discovered that their attitude differs little from E. B. White's. John Cheever called the attempt to write seriously "quite a dangerous career." Katherine Anne Porter thought that for writers, courage was "the first essential."

Before I began writing for a living, it hadn't occurred to me that courage was part of the job description. I knew this calling took skill, imagination, and persistence, and hoped I had these qualities. By working at a newspaper I'd learned some basics of my craft. With savings and a few contacts among editors, I set out to be a freelance writer. I outfitted myself with a thesaurus, a style manual, and a brand-new Smith-Corona typewriter. Now it was just a matter of getting down to business. Or so I thought.

Only after my tenth sleepless night did it dawn on me that there might be more to this business than recording good words on paper. By the time I started my first book, there was no escaping the fact that anxiety had elbowed its way into my office to sit beside me, scrutinizing every word I wrote. Much of this anxiety showed up in disguise. It expressed itself as stomach trouble, irritability, and restlessness. During toss-and-turn nights I'd jot notes on a pad beside my bed. (Like marijuana-inspired brilliance, such notes were seldom of any use in the light of day.) Seven-day workweeks became routine as I tried to build walls of research and rhetoric strong enough to protect me from marauding critics. When a friend offered me a relaxing massage to ease my obvious tension, I turned the offer down out of fear that getting too relaxed might keep me from finishing my book. I had trouble even *thinking* about anything other than getting the book done. Taking a weekend off or even spending an evening with friends might break the writing spell forever, I feared. Then I might never return to my desk. I would be revealed as an impostor: someone who said he could write a book but couldn't.

I did finish that book (*We, the Lonely People: Searching for Community*) but doubted I'd do another. Why endure such trauma again? Yet within the year I was writing a second book, and three years later, a third. I've now been through this process eight times. Along the way, I've learned three things. One is that I'll survive; finish the book and live to write another. Second, I'll regain my sanity (such as it is). Finally, I've learned that a rising tide of anxiety isn't necessarily bad. It's a sign that I'm getting serious. Nervousness keeps me alert. Fear forces me to focus and to work longer hours. Restless nights mean I'm gaining momentum. The end is in sight. Getting there isn't always pleasant. Neither is running in a marathon. Or staging a play. Or climbing a mountain. All such activities take courage. And all reward those who complete them not only with an unparalleled feeling of achievement but with a thrilling sense of adventure along the way.

Writers sometimes compare themselves to explorers.

John Ashbery said that for him, the excitement of writing poetry lay in going to new places. "Voyages of exploration," is what Malcolm Cowley called novel writing. Any writing worth doing is a trek into the unknown. Writers never know where their pen or keyboard will take them. "You go in with a certain fear and trembling," said James Baldwin of writing books. "You know one thing. You know you will not be the same person when this voyage is over. But you don't know what's going to happen to you between getting on the boat and stepping off."

The longer I write, the more my admiration has grown for those who set out on this journey. They are apprehensive and should be. Writing is a daring act. Any time we put so much as a word on paper we're in jeopardy. (What if someone thinks we could have chosen a better one?) Whoever writes for public scrutiny is subject to a form of what psychologists call "performance anxiety." Polls routinely confirm that public speaking is our number-one fear. (Dying ranks sixth, according to one such poll.) Writing is merely public speaking on paper, but to a much larger audience. For some, writing to publish is even more daunting than speaking in public. Spoken words blow away in the wind. Published ones last as long as the paper on which they're printed.

A psychologist I know named Brian makes a good living giving lectures. In the world of public speakers, writing a book is considered a first-rate marketing tool. An author who speaks has far more panache than a speaker alone. Brian knows this. He wants desperately to write a book, and not just as a marketing tool. There are things Brian has to say that he'd like people to read: about the environment, family issues, and social ethics. So far he hasn't been able to put them on paper. This man can electrify thousands of listeners when he gives a keynote address. He does so dozens of times a year. But whenever Brian approaches a typewriter, his fingers rebel. They refuse to convey messages from his brain to the paper.

Brian has lots of company. The trail of literary history is littered with those who fell along the way because the anxiety of trying to write paralyzed their hand. Many nonwriting writers are gifted. The best writers I know teach school and sell real estate. Some still plan to write "someday." Others have given up altogether. Their block lies not with their ability or skill but with their nerve.

"You need a certain amount of nerve to be a writer," said Margaret Atwood, "an almost physical nerve, the kind you need to walk a log across a river." Few of her colleagues would disagree. Yet too many writers think it's their shameful little secret that they're scared. That's simply not so. Fear is felt by writers at every level. Anxiety accompanies the first word they put on paper and the last. "I write in terror," admitted Cynthia Ozick. "I have to talk myself into bravery with every sentence, sometimes every syllable."

Its psychic demands make writing an exercise in courage little different from climbing a sheer granite cliff or skiing down a steep slope. This often surprises new writers. No literary neophyte doubts that hard work lies ahead. Most realize that certain skills must be mastered to compose a coherent text. They hope their intellectual gifts will allow them to produce work of substance. The real shock is discovering how demanding writing is not just of their skill, talent, and work ethic but of their valor.

The Great Unspoken

My friend Cal recently completed a short story. Cal had taken a writing class, gotten tutoring from his teacher, and joined a writers' group. More important, he wrote. The results were promising. I've read worse stories in print. Would he try to get his published? Cal said he was thinking about it. He'd gone so far as to collect the names of magazines but hadn't sent his story to any of them.

Why not? I asked.

"I'm too scared."

During a quarter century as a writer and teacher of writing, I've heard hundreds of variations on this theme. An inability to write, finish a piece of writing, or put completed writing in the mail is routine among those who want to see their words in print. If they realized that all writers are anxious—but that writing fears are predictable and manageable—perhaps more discouraged writers would be writing today. Although crippling anxieties are as much a part of the writing process as punctuation, they also are a Great Unspoken.

The huge database Nexis has only twelve references to *writing anxiety*. By contrast, Nexis has well over a thousand citations for the term *writer's block*. There's a reason for this. Calling an inability to write a "block" suggests there's just some obstruction down the line that can be cleared with a literary Roto-Rooter. According to one school of thought, writing blocks are due primarily to faulty technique. In other words, blocked writers simply haven't learned their literary lessons. That's a promising premise. The notion that writing problems can be solved by learning how to choose better words and move more smoothly from one paragraph to the next is reassuring. "One more course and I'll be writing away."

But writing problems aren't that easily solved. Few result from ignorance alone. Most writers know the basics of their craft: show, don't tell; use active verbs; be sparing with adjectives and adverbs; make effective use of detail. It's important to learn and relearn these lessons. Yet there's a limit to how much mastering writing rules can do to improve prose or poetry. In the long run, learning techniques does far less to improve our writing than finding the will, the nerve, the *guts* to put on paper what we really want to say.

Unfortunately, there is not much help available to do this. Most writing courses and books only strike fear a glancing blow. They rarely address the crippling inhibitions that keep even gifted writers from getting material out of their head, onto paper, and into the mail. According to Bonnie Friedman, a graduate of the University of Iowa Writers' Workshop, her seminars there dealt with words on the page but not how to find them. Among the key questions she and her fellow students never asked were: How to write despite fear? Where to find courage? "*Courage* is from the word for heart," said Friedman in her book, *Writing Past Dark*. "School had little to do with heart, and everything to do with technical perfection."

Even programs and books that do acknowledge how daunting writing can be usually advise anxious writers to just roll up their sleeves, sharpen their pencils, and get busy. The obvious advice for anyone intimidated by writing fears is: "Don't be scared. What are you afraid of? Just do it!" Such exhortations are offered most freely by those who aren't up on the high wire themselves (i.e., teachers, editors, critics).

But there are genuine, serious, and understandable reasons to be anxious about writing. Advising writers to ignore their anxiety and forge ahead is like telling a ten-year-old who's about to get a shot, "There's nothing to be scared of." That kid knows better. So do writers.

When I lecture on writing fears, listeners usually sit up straight and pay close attention. This has nothing to do with my speaking ability and everything to do with their personal stake in this topic. Most know exactly what I'm talking about. They know because they're so eager to write and so anxious about the prospect. At the same time, they can't imagine that anyone else feels the same way, let alone published authors. As we've seen, writing fears are nearly universal. But because they're seldom discussed openly, we feel alone with ours. Much of the paralyzing fear of writing is due to the fact that its power isn't dissipated by opening windows to air this subject out.

Courage vs. Fearlessness

This book deals openly with writing fears because these fears are so seldom acknowledged, leaving each of us to feel we're the only one who has them. Considering directly how scary writing can be, and why, can do more to facilitate writing than a dozen classes on technique. All writers must confront their fears eventually. The sooner they do this, the better their work will be.

Finding the courage to write does not involve erasing or "conquering" one's fears. Working writers aren't those who have eliminated their anxiety. They are the ones who keep scribbling while their heart races and their stomach churns, and who mail manuscripts with trembling fingers.

The key difference between writers who are paralyzed by fear and those who are merely terrified is that—like E. B. White—the latter come to terms with their anxieties. They learn how to keep writing even as fear tries to yank their hand from the page. They find the courage to write.

We often use the terms *fearless* and *courageous* as if they were synonyms. In fact they're closer to antonyms. Mark Twain defined *courage* as "resistance to fear, mastery of fear—not absence of fear." General Omar Bradley called it "the capacity to perform properly even when scared half to death." In *The Courage to Create*, Rollo May pointed out that existential philosophers such as Kierkegaard, Nietzsche, Camus, and Sartre all concurred that courage didn't mean the absence of despair; rather it meant "the capacity to move ahead *in spite of despair.*"

Trying to deny, avoid, numb, or eradicate the fear of writing is neither possible nor desirable. Anxiety is not only an inevitable part of the writing process but a necessary part. *If you're not scared, you're not writing.* No message in this book is more important. A state of anxiety is the writer's natural habitat. Yet those who live there are seldom bold. Bullfighting Hemingways and Africa-settling Dinesens are the exception among writers. Most seek adventure only in their own imaginations. Like most of us, they're brave here, timid there, trying to muddle through, to sneak enough good words onto paper before a surge of anxiety erases their literary disk. At the same time, they're driven to seek attention and must peddle their wares to the public. This leads to a psychic conundrum that writers often note in themselves; "a combination of an almost obscene self-confidence and an ongoing terror," John Barth called it.

To love writing, fear writing, and pray for the courage to

write is no contradiction. Nor is it paradoxical to be both scared and thrilled by the prospect. Kids on skateboards and writers at their desk know the same thing: fear fuels excitement. Writing is both frightening and exhilarating. It couldn't be one without the other. The best writers exploit fear's energy to billow the sails of their imaginations. They convert anxiety into enthusiasm and an unparalleled source of energy.

The Power of Positive Anxiety

In my writing classes, there's one student I always look for eagerly. It's usually a woman. She sits close to the door, to make for an easy getaway. This student seldom says much. She often accosts me after class to say she's about to drop out. Why? "I'm too scared," the woman tells me. "I can't do it." I always urge that student to stick around. I know she'll produce some of our best work.

During one workshop, a computer programmer named Julie kept warning me that she was about to jump in her car and drive back to Pittsburgh. Luckily for us, she didn't. When assigned to write a profile, Julie spent two hours circling the home of an artist she'd chosen to portray, working up the courage to knock on his door. The visit she described was filled with the spilled turpentine, half-squeezed paint tubes, partly smoked reefers, and empty matchbooks that brought her subject's surroundings to life. Julie wrote about this artist's studio with the exquisite awareness of a victim in a torture chamber. To her, that's just what it felt like.

Students such as Julie have already won half the battle: they've lifted the lid of their defenses to let anxiety rise to the surface. If they can then use that anxiety to fertilize their work, writing may be in their future. A willingness to confront the fear of putting words on paper is an excellent basis for becoming a writer. "My students often told me they didn't have anything to say," reported the University of New Hampshire's Donald Murray in his book *Shoptalk.* "They were silent. Empty. They felt anxiety. Panic. Terror. 'Good,' I'd answer. 'You are a writer. You are at the place from which writing comes.' "

We can't eradicate our writing fears. Nor would we want to. They're what make writing so challenging and satisfying. That is this book's premise: that anxiety is a normal, manageable, and even useful part of the writing process. The book is divided into two parts. The first part considers different types of writing anxiety, analyzes their causes, and assesses how fear influences our work. The second part includes suggestions for the ways not only to write in the face of fear but to enlist fear's energy in the cause of becoming a better writer.

So far, we've talked mostly in general terms about writing fears. In the next chapter, let's get more specific. What is it exactly that makes writing so demanding of our courage?

2

Points of Courage

> I always have a sense of trembling,
> but so does a compass, after all.
> —*Jerzy Kosinski*

*W*henever I start writing a book, my fears follow a predictable path. First I'm scared that I won't finish it; that I'll be exposed as a fraud who conned a publisher into thinking he could write a book. When I do complete a manuscript, I'm afraid my editor won't accept it. If my editor does accept the manuscript, I'm worried that critics will hate it. If critics don't hate it, I'm sure no one will buy my book. And even if readers do buy my book, there's the danger that they won't like what they read. They might find it laughable. Worst of all, someone I know may ridicule my efforts. These are the types of fears that keep me, and anyone who presumes to write for public consumption, awake at night.

When I ticked off this list of fears for a group discussing writing anxiety, other participants—who ranged from aspiring to published authors—had little trouble expanding the list. A high school teacher said she was scared to mail any of the poems she wrote at night. If they came back, the teacher explained, "then I'm no longer Emily Dickinson. The dream has been demolished."

A college writing coach noted the paradox that she could help students get over their fear of writing but couldn't get over her own. "I don't believe anyone who says my writing's any good," said the coach. "I'm looking for the 'but' in anything anyone says."

"My major fear," agreed a doctor, "is that I really can't be any good. That if people say they like my writing, they're just being polite. That they don't see how bad it really is. But if I submit anything for publication, *they'll* tell me the truth."

A writing-blocked businessman recalled how excruciating writing had been for him in college; so excruciating that he didn't write much for twenty years. Only now does he realize how much anxiety was involved. "At the time I didn't sense it as fear," the businessman explained. "I only sensed it as hating it."

One member of the group had already published a book and was about to publish another. The only time she wasn't afraid, this author told the others, was after she'd begun but before she had to produce anything. What was she afraid of? "My most pronounced fear is that I'm a one-book writer," said the author. "Then, my fear is—when I stop giving this book my attention—what next? Will I have anything else to write about? Will I be able to write another book? And on and on and on."

The list of writing anxieties is a long one. Think of them as courage points. They can change over the course of a project. In this chapter we will consider specific fears that accompany the writing process, from the time we first start thinking about "doing some writing" through completion of a manuscript, its submission, and the war waged between pride and panic as we hold a first copy of our first book.

Can I Pull It Off?

As a frustrated young writer, Gail Godwin was married briefly to a British psychiatrist. His therapeutic technique was to repeat a key question until he got a true answer. Godwin credited this technique with forcing her to face what had kept her from writing the novels she so desperately wanted to write. In a cathartic moment, the two had this exchange:

> "Why can't you be a writer?" he asked.
>
> "Because . . . I don't know . . . something keeps getting in the way."
>
> "I see. But why can't you be a writer?"
>
> "Because! I told you, something never quite . . . jells."
>
> "Hmm. But . . . why can't you be a writer?"
>
> "Oh, I don't know. Look at my mother. She wrote and wrote and wrote. And nobody ever published her novels. Heartbreaking."
>
> "Yes. But why can't *you* be a writer?"
>
> "When I write in my journals, it's fine. You know it is, you bastard, you've read them yourself, without my permission. They flow, they're real. Whereas, the minute I put on my writing hat and sit down to 'write a story,' I bore myself to death. I kill it, I kill the whole thing."
>
> "I see. Why can't you be a writer, then?"
>
> "Because . . . because . . . OH, GOD! Because

I'm afraid I might fail! . . . Good God, that's it!
That's it, you know. What a spineless, lily-livered
fraidy-cat I have been!"

Like the young Gail Godwin, fledgling writers are seldom
clear about what's scaring them; they just know they're
scared. If articulated at all, their fear is usually along the lines
of "I'm not sure I can pull it off." Or, "Suppose I don't like
what I write?" Or, "I've got so much riding on being a *writer*,
and now I've got to put words on paper and we're all going to
find out, aren't we? Do I really have anything to say? Can I
fill the page with more than gibberish?"

Among rookies and veterans alike, the most basic writing
fear is of simply not being up to the task. *Now that I've told
the world, and myself, that I can write, suppose it turns out that I
can't?* Even the prolific Anthony Burgess said he thought
constantly about giving up writing because of the debilitat-
ing fear that his work wasn't good enough.

Just thinking about being a writer can be scary (as well as
thrilling; the two tend to go hand in hand). Saying—even
to yourself—"I'm a writer," or "I'm going to be a writer,"
or even "I guess I'll do some writing now," feels presumptuous; like a five-year-old playing make-believe for be-
mused grown-ups. Isabel Allende had to publish three
novels before she felt comfortable putting *writer* rather than
housewife in the space for *Occupation* when filling out a form.
Writer was "such a *big* word," explained Allende. One reason playwright A. R. Gurney taught college for so long was
that he found it easier to call himself a teacher than a writer.
The turning point came when a novelist he knew chastised
Gurney for hedging his bet. "You gotta start calling yourself
a writer," said this friend, "you gotta start thinking of

yourself as a writer. You're never gonna get anywhere if you don't take yourself seriously."

I Can't Write About That!

Once we've resolved to write (at least on a contingency basis), the next question is, About what? Answering that deceptively simple question can itself take courage. Like a tongue searching out cracked fillings, an inner scan for writing ideas makes a beeline for tender parts of our psyche. That's where the most potent material hides out. We all know what we'd *really* like to write about. But it's exceedingly hard—nearly impossible—to find the courage to expose such topics to readers. (Should I write about feeling too fat to please my mother? It might kill her. How about the time I got caught shoplifting? Uncle Horace would never speak to me again. Maybe I could plumb my fantasies of making love on Principal Hargrove's desk—but only when I'm ready to leave town.)

Writers are always hungry for compelling topics to explore. The problem is that the best ones are mortifying. A warm flush of embarrassment is like a dowsing rod pointing its quivering tip right at deep wells of rich material. When our cheeks feel hot with chagrin, we've probably hit a gusher. "The best work that anybody ever writes," said Arthur Miller, "is the work that is on the verge of embarrassing him, always."

One student I taught in a night course was a single father who spent most class sessions hiding behind dark sunglasses. Bo's usual garb was a black silk jacket with a fire-breathing dragon on the back. His writing consisted primarily of polemics about a wide range of social ills. The attention

Bo's classmates paid to these essays was polite but dutiful. Finally I asked him if he wouldn't mind trying something else. I didn't want to change his ideology, I explained, but simply wondered if he might spread his wings a little; try to write something that would touch our heart as well as our social conscience.

Bo did. His next piece of writing was a poignant, ten-page depiction of one sleepless night in the life of a man whose wife had recently moved in with a younger lover, leaving her husband alone to raise their four children. Bo wove the warp of this man's tossing and turning with the woof of a detailed look at the demands of single fatherhood. With this risky, gripping piece of writing, he finally reached his teacher and classmates.

My own most successful book grew out of the anxiety I felt while reading an invitation to a high school class reunion. God, I thought, is anyone else this anxious at the thought of going back to face their classmates? Why am I? The reasons were painfully obvious. Most grew out of the fear that if I returned to the scene of my adolescent humiliations, they'd begin all over again. Would I still be tongue-tied around Donna Darnelle? Would Howie Dubin want to resume our fistfight over Roz Rosenberg? And what if Carla Rollins showed up? Would she smile indulgently about the night she invited me over because her parents were gone and I was too timid to go?

Were these things worth writing about? My mind tried to change the subject. I kept having to wrestle it back to the reunion. Although I couldn't attend that gathering, which was held in mid-December, a continent away, I did write a book about the stranglehold adolescent memories have on adult sensibilities. Writing *Is There Life After High School?*

involved going to other people's reunions, which was fun, and spending a day back at my own high school, which wasn't. In the gym that day I found myself trying to impress Coach Carlisle. Carlisle had cut me from the basketball team twelve years before. I hoped Coach would notice the improvement in my jump shot. He didn't. Back in the hallways, I quickly remembered how to assess others by the books they carried. (*Bookkeeping*. Commercial course. Not my type.) At lunch I didn't know where to sit. I thought about asking to join Susie, the junior who'd chatted with me in line, but demurred. Surely she'd say no. Susie came to my rescue by inviting me to sit at her table. After school I walked her partway home, past the practicing football players whom I still envied.

The whole day was a total embarrassment. It forced me to consider the possibility that I hadn't matured a whit since leaving high school. Yet out of that excruciating few hours grew a piece of writing that remains one of my favorites. In it, I was working very close to my obsessions.

That's the bind writers face: their best ideas are personal, candid, and deeply felt. Yet such ideas make them feel subnaked before the world. It's as if not just their clothes but their skin has been stripped away so that readers can get a better look at their entrails. One reason we routinely turn away from topics we'd most like to write about (without always realizing what we're doing) is that they're so dangerously revealing.

One writer friend of mine was a great raconteur about his early life as a half-Jew raised among neo-Nazi relatives. None of this showed up in his short stories, which he ironically called "evasive fiction." Another friend wrote plays about everything but his fascinating years as an unmarried teenage father in the 1950s. That topic, he told me, was just too "touchy." I've heard variations on this theme time and again: not daring to dive into passions and come up with pearls to put on the page. "I couldn't write about *that*" is the usual explanation. But *that* is what we write about with greatest intensity. And *that* is what readers most want to read about.

My mother—a sometime writer—often told her family rich, sometimes scandalous stories about growing up in Philadelphia in the 1920s. These stories featured the speakeasies she began patronizing at the age of fourteen, and her practice of rubbing cigarette ashes onto her eighth-grade schoolwork so the teachers would know whom they were up against. One relative of Mom's spent years wandering in crowds looking for the face of a son who'd run away. Another relative—the mysterious "Tanta Carolina"—was said to have run a brothel in Saigon before returning to Bucharest to become a fortune-teller late last century. When girls in my mother's family wore too much makeup, they were warned that they'd end up "just like Tanta Carolina." None of these stories ever showed up in print under Mom's byline. Instead she produced essays on the need for disarmament and stories illustrating themes of universal brotherhood. As a result, my mother's written oeuvre was far less interesting than her spoken one, and she enjoyed nothing like the literary success she'd dreamed of since childhood.

Those who *tell* stories better than they write them are the bane of editors. Editors dread wasting time on captivating talkers whose words lose their fizz on the page. Obviously, writing skills transcend conversational skills. But the drama and flair we bring to *telling* stories is too often lost once our words are nailed down on paper. Most of us converse better than we write because we feel so much less vulnerable when addressing a limited number of ears. While talking, we can alter material or adjust our delivery in response to cues from others. If things get out of hand, we can change the subject altogether. Even when they bomb, spoken words float off toward Mars. They can always be denied. "That isn't what I said!" is a great court of last resort. But words we've committed to paper can be held in evidence against us as long as that paper exists. Is it any wonder that we're scared to make this commitment?

Page Fright

All my life, I've been frightened at the moment I sit down to write.

—*Gabriel García Márquez*

. . . . .

It's really scary just getting to the desk—we're talking now five hours. My mouth gets dry, my heart beats fast. I react psychologically the way other people react when the plane loses an engine.

—*Fran Lebowitz*

. . . . .

I suffer as always from the fear of putting down the first line. It is amazing the terrors, the magics, the prayers, the straightening shyness that assails one.

—*John Steinbeck*

Blank pages inspire me with terror.
—*Margaret Atwood*

This is page fright: a fear of confronting the blank page. Page fright is the literary counterpart of stage fright. Even experienced writers approach each writing session apprehensive that nothing—or junk, or scary stuff—will come out. Facing a blank page or computer screen is the moment of truth. It's alarming to sit before a cleared desk with nothing but your thoughts (or lack thereof) to record. The time for dreaming, talking, and planning is over. Now you must *write*. At that moment the page can seem like a huge literary black hole that you must somehow fill with tiny words. As one fledgling writer asked me in a midmorning phone plea: "How do you *start*?"

The best time of writing is before any words have been committed to paper; when all is prospect, clear in one's mind, and clearly brilliant. The problems begin when one attempts to record that vision on paper. No matter how gifted and experienced the writer, this simply can't be done. "I have never yet succeeded in perfectly reproducing what was on my mind," admitted Paul Laurence Dunbar. The writing that shows up on paper is rarely as good as the writing in one's head. Anthony Burgess thought every book was a failure from the moment its first sentence was written, because this sentence destroyed forever the dream of what that book might be. "The awful thing about the first sentence of any book," agreed Tom Wolfe, "is that as soon as you've written it you realize this piece of work is not going to be the great thing that you envision. It can't be." The page has a mind of its own.

The Paper Partner

Once writers commit words to paper, they're no longer sole proprietors of their own business. They've taken the page on as a partner. This partner can be as surly, insolent, and pigheaded as a fourteen-year-old who's been told to clean his room. The author's new partner has ideas of his own about where the enterprise should be headed. Rather than change direction, he will dig in his heels every step of the way. "Feral" is the way Annie Dillard has depicted him. In Dillard's experience, any piece of writing quickly reverts to an untamed state. Over time, it becomes like a lion cub growing into fierce maturity. "You must visit it every day and reassert your mastery over it," said Dillard. "If you skip a day, you are, quite rightly, afraid to open the door to its room. You enter its room with bravura, holding a chair at the thing and shouting, 'Simba!' "

Fingers that clutch a pen or tap a keyboard go their own way with blithe disregard for the person who thinks he's doing the writing. What results might not resemble at all what a writer sat down to produce. Any story is always on the verge of careening off the page as it comes to life. "People get married, and I didn't realize they were engaged," said Pat Conroy. "People die in these novels and I'm surprised. They take on this little subterranean life of their own."

For those who become writers to create a world they can rule, as many do, it takes courage to relinquish that power, as all must. Writers typically create fictional worlds because they find the real one unappealing. They want to produce a fantasy realm more to their liking, one that feels less anxious. Far from easing their anxiety, however, this unruly new world can enhance it. The writer may not like all the characters who show up on his page. Some may frighten him. Worse yet, he may have to hurt characters he does like. James Jones once greeted a laundryman at his door with tears streaming down his face because of the mayhem he was inflicting upon his fictional offspring. Robert Stone couldn't write for a month after killing a character to whom he'd grown attached.

Doing bad things to good characters is painful and scary. Real courage is called for here, to face the demands writing can place on one's soul. Hardest of all is to accept that the world one has created won't be as good as the world one dreamed of writing about. It never is. "Every book," said Iris Murdoch, "is the wreck of a perfect idea." Once this is clear, it's easy to panic, get blocked, or to give up writing altogether as an impossible dream. One thing that separates would-be writers from working writers is that the latter know their work will never match their dreams. Nonwriters typically vow that if they can't make the book on paper look as good as the one in their head, they just won't write it. Working writers know this is an impossible dream and settle for the closest facsimile.

"All of us failed to match our dream of perfection," said William Faulkner. "So I rate us on the basis of our splendid failure to do the impossible. In my opinion, if I could write all my work again, I am convinced that I would do it better, which is the healthiest condition for an artist. That's why he keeps on working, trying again; he believes each time that this time he will do it, bring it off. Of course he won't, which is why this condition is healthy. Once he did it, once he matched the work to the image, the dream, nothing would remain but to cut his throat, jump off the other side of that pinnacle of perfection into suicide."

Faulkner had the courage to accept that flawed work (flawed to him, anyway) was better than none at all. So do the best writers in general. They must. No book on paper can ever match the one in one's head. What Paul Valéry said of poems is true of all writing: it is never completed, only abandoned. Once writers realize this, they're faced with a cruel choice: shall they leave their premature baby in a basket on some publisher's doorstep, or shall they hide that poor child in the basement and turn away from writing as an impossible dream?

Evicting the Baby

According to Kathy Trocheck, many of her fellow *Atlanta Journal and Constitution* reporters had novels in their computers just as she did. Their dream of getting them published was little different from hers. The difference was, said Trocheck, "I *wanted* it. I wanted it badly enough to ship my novel off to a publisher. Which is a scary thing to do. It's much easier to write a manuscript and stick it in a bottom desk drawer. It's very scary to stick it in the mail." Trocheck did, and went on to publish the first three novels in an ongoing mystery series for HarperCollins. She no longer works as a reporter.

It seems self-evident, but isn't always, that writers must send their work to publishers. This act involves such high stakes that some just can't. A key moment that distinguishes would-be writers from those who publish is the one when fingers open to let an envelope holding a manuscript disappear into the dark abyss of a mailbox. Suppose it comes back? One way to preserve a fantasy of becoming a great writer is by never testing that fantasy; by being a writer of great promise whose best work is always yet to come. This is why so many manuscripts are never seen by anyone but trusted friends and relatives. Robert Heinlein estimated that only a small percentage of the vast minority of writers who actually complete a manuscript ever mail one. "Writers—all writers—including scarred old professionals—are inordinately fond of their brainchildren," observed the author of *Stranger in a Strange Land*. "They would rather see their firstborn child ravaged by wolves than suffer the pain of having a manuscript rejected. So instead they read their manuscripts aloud to spouses and long-suffering friends."

For those who do mail their work, the subsequent period has a tangy flavor. Far from the elation they anticipate—the delirious joy of triumph and release—authors of newly mailed manuscripts typically slip into a postpartum funk. Toni Morrison described this mood as feeling that something was missing in her life; her characters, their company, the sense of possibility they offered. No matter how unruly a child a manuscript becomes, working on it gives shape to a writer's day. Anxiety about rearing that child is a familiar companion. The literary offspring may turn into a disobedient brat, but it's the author's brat. Writing comes from inside an author as surely as a physical progeny does. Once that child has been sent off to live with strangers, alarming questions plague the author. Will these strangers care for her? Love her? Attempt to do her harm? Abuse her, even?

These are troubling questions. They give the post-submission-period a manic-depressive quality. "Letting go of it seemed to leave me without purpose," said Larry L. King after he mailed the manuscript of his first novel, *The One-Eyed Man*. "I was restless, glum, irritable. I have since learned that a certain amount of those old postcreative glums are inevitable and normal. After one has lived with a writing project for months or years, finishing it brings one a quick burst of elation and then that unnerving feeling of being at loose ends. A deep-blue funky melancholy soon follows."

Like most new writers, I was startled to discover how quickly I slipped into a black trough of despair after mailing my first book manuscript. I'd expected nothing but sunny days once this guest who'd overstayed his welcome was sent packing. The second time it happened I was less surprised but no less dismayed to find myself moping about after a completed manuscript flew the coop. All the fun times I'd promised myself—weekends off, trips to town, lunch with friends—lost their appeal. I still wasn't convinced, however, that such a response wasn't unique to each of these two projects. By the third, fourth, and fifth postpartum depressions there was no avoiding the fact that despair followed manuscript completion as inevitably as darkness followed sundown. But I also learned ways to cope with that despair. Sometimes I'd take a trip out of town. In other cases I'd throw myself into long-postponed physical labor around the house. The most effective antidote of all, however, was to make sure that I had a new project to tackle after no more than a weekend's respite; preferably a new book.

When the industrious Anthony Trollope finished a novel before fulfilling his day's writing quota, he'd simply scribble "Chapter One" on a fresh sheet of paper and begin a new one. More often, authors of newly completed manuscripts putter about, sleep late, brood, and try the patience of long-ignored friends with frantic phone calls as they wonder whether their editor likes what they've written (or is even reading it). Sometimes they even call and ask. "I became just like all the writers who have given me grief," a book editor told me after she sent an article to a magazine. "I kept calling and calling and asking for a response. I was *so* anxious."

Galley Jitters

Any editor I've known who's crossed the literary Rubicon to publish something under her own name has gone just as goofy as any other writer, if not more so (because she's so startled and embarrassed). Editors usually are on the other side of the desk, trying to soothe the nerves of panicky authors while clucking their mental tongues about what scaredy-cats writers can be. Editors who write are like doctors who get sick and find themselves behaving no differently from the thousands of patients they've patronized over the years.

I once came upon the former editor in chief of a publishing house clutching a Federal Express envelope with all the ease of a father carrying his firstborn. Only he looked far less happy than a new father. "What's that?" I asked, pointing to the envelope. "Galley proofs," he murmured. "Of my memoirs." "How are you feeling?" I asked. "*Pure* anxiety," replied the ex-editor. The next day I walked with him to a library where he was about to look up the spelling of a river near his hometown. By now the face of the editor-turned-author had grown pasty and was creased with gulleys of tension. "I'm going crazy," he told me. "Most writers I've ever dealt with are nut cases. Now I'm that nut case. Now I'm going to the library to check the spelling of fucking *Monongahela*."

This editor was discovering what most writers already know: how unnerving a moment it can be to "check galleys." That's a writer's last opportunity to make sure the child's face is washed, her clothes clean, her shoelaces tied. Eudora Welty thought galley jitters might result from the fact that seeing her words in print for the first time forced the writer to read them more with the cold eye of a reader than with the maternal eye of a mother. "It gives me a terrible sense of exposure," Welty said of this transition, "as if I'd gotten sunburned."

I find that checking galleys is excruciating. Until then, vexing writing problems can always be brushed aside by saying, "I'll take care of that later." Now there is no later. Galleys offer the *last chance* to make changes (i.e, protect one's self from eternal humiliation). Lawrence Durrell found that he could only look at galley proofs after fortifying himself with aspirin. If changes were necessary, he asked someone else to make them. "I don't know why," said Durrell of his horror at reading galleys. "I just have a nausea about it. Perhaps when one day I get something I really do like, I won't have to take aspirin."

Early in her career, novelist Sharon Sheehe Stark had a short story accepted by a literary magazine. A few months later she met that magazine's editor at a cocktail party during a writers' conference. He gave Stark what looked like galley proofs of her story, which was scheduled to appear in his magazine's next issue. Leaving the party, Stark went to her room and began going over the galleys. After admiring their pristine whiteness, she started drawing spiderwebs of lines from good words in the text to better ones in the margins. She crossed out entire paragraphs and rewrote others. This work consumed the entire night. The next morning, weary but proud, Stark handed her revised galleys to the editor. The man was horrified. As if to a child, he explained that what he'd given her weren't galleys; they were *camera-ready page proofs*. Although a nearby book editor told him that "only a nut would give a writer something he didn't want written on," the magazine editor was not mollified. Stark's story never ran.

Editors find writers who are intimidated by galleys a major pain. Such authors pose a serious threat to production schedules. Writers see a different picture altogether. The danger they see is one of having imperfections preserved in amber as long as a single copy of their work exists.

What editors don't understand, and can't—until they publish something under their own name—is how much danger writers feel they're in. To writers on the front lines, it's easy to conclude that if every phrase is polished, each word perfect, all commas in place, they're protected. A bulletproof vest of style has been donned. Any editor who asks a well-defended writer to hurry up with galleys, or to change so much as a semicolon in a manuscript, can seem like an officer ordering a soldier under fire to climb out of a well-fortified trench and start digging a new one.

Writers work under constant threat of public ridicule and rejection. Editors are protected by a shield of public anonymity. Their names are generally known only to a few colleagues. It's not that editors aren't afraid and don't take risks. But their risks aren't taken in full view of the reading public. To those about to go over the top into an artillery barrage fired by reviewers, booksellers, and readers, editors are rear-guard generals who plan battles for writers to fight. As Fred Allen asked after a team of pencil-wielding editors had their way with one of his radio scripts, "Where were you guys when the page was blank?"

Advance-Copy Anxiety

When Sherri Szeman opened the package that contained an advance copy of her first novel, *The Kommandant's Mistress*, she panicked. "I was *so* scared," recalled Szeman. "My book was about to be sent out in the world. I was afraid that people would read it and say, 'What the hell does she think she's doing?' I called my editor and told her how I felt. She said it doesn't get any better. That this happens with each book."

To nonwriters, receiving a first copy of your own book would seem to be a moment of unalloyed ecstasy. (My book! I did it! I'm a published writer! Me! I've reached the promised land!) In fact, examining the first copy of your book is a far more mixed experience. On the one hand, proof now rests in your hand that you indeed wrote a book. This exciting thought lasts for about six seconds. Then the mind turns elsewhere: Couldn't my publisher have found a better typeface for the jacket? Next time, I'm going to hire a professional photographer to take a good author picture. I wonder what Mom's gonna think when she reads the rape scene. I wonder how long it'll be before my book shows up on remainder tables. I wonder if it's going to get panned. I wonder if anyone will read it at all.

Washington Irving once confided to a friend that he dreaded opening an advance copy of one of his books. Rather than spasms of joy, he felt tremblings of fear as he recalled the book's weaknesses, the many places where he might have written better. This is a common reaction when examining a new book with one's name on the spine. Anything wrong with that book—by the author's hand or its publisher's—is now on public display. Any mistakes a writer's eye catches are there forever (or at least until the publisher decides to do a corrected second printing). For me, first-book experiences have included turning one over to discover a grainy, uncropped photograph of the author with his shirt not tucked in neatly. That picture still makes me wince. Another book of mine included a factual error in the flap copy. My last book not only had Betty Grable's name misspelled as *Gable* (mea culpa) but it had her starring in the movie *Incendiary Blonde* (mea secunda culpa). As several readers brought to my attention, Betty Hutton starred in that movie.

Such goofs, and worse, are surprisingly common. The talent coordinator for a television show told me that she'd booked more than one author whose name was misspelled on his book jacket. The venerable Library of America misspelled Herman Melville's name as *Meville* on the title page of one volume of his collected works. According to the dust jacket of Bernard Malamud's *God's Grace*, Malamud wrote John Updike's novel *The Centaur*. Several hundred copies of John O'Hara's *Butterfield 8* were bound inside the covers of a John Wesley biography. In the first edition of Henry James's novel *The Ambassadors*, chapter 28 followed chapter 29.

I've read books whose tables of contents didn't match their chapters; that had pages bound upside down; that lacked entire sections or had two duplicated. The final section of David Bradley's *Chaneysville Incident* was omitted from my copy. I started Bradley's suspenseful novel while vacationing on an island, then had to wait until I left the island to find out what happened. Is it any wonder that authors scrutinize newly published books with as much panic as pride?

Postpublication Panic

For many authors, the period following publication is when *real* nerve is called for, to contend with the loss of control they feel. "Writing is a lot about control," explained Richard Louv, author of four nonfiction books, including *Childhood's Future*. "Once the book goes out the door, you're confronted with things you can't control. You enter the totally chaotic world of publishing. To me that takes more courage than writing."

Publishers generally don't let authors in on plans to market their book (often because there aren't any). Like surrogate mothers who produce a healthy baby, writers who deliver an acceptable manuscript are thought to have done their job. Unless they are needed to make publicity appearances, publishers tend to regard such authors as a potential nuisance. Those who edit, promote, and market books talk to one another daily. They speak the same language. An author's voice rudely interrupts their conversations with its whiny, anxious tone.

After reading the manuscript of T. Gertler's novel *Elbowing the Seducer*, her editor at Houghton Mifflin made fourteen copies to circulate in-house. To publishing cognoscenti, such a move is good news. It indicates enthusiasm. When the editor told Gertler what he'd done, however, she panicked. "I'm very secretive," the first-time author told him. "I thought—'all those people looking at it!' " Responded her editor, "That's the concept, Trudy—anybody who wants to can see it."

One might imagine that writers wouldn't act like such frightened children if they were more familiar with the ways of publishers. That's a dubious assumption. Even the voice of publishing insiders grows anxious when a book of their own is about to appear in bookstores. As his first novel (*Works of Genius*) was about to be published, veteran editor Richard Marek said he felt scared as well as happy because he was about to be subjected to a kind of exposure he never got as an editor. The word *exposure* comes up a lot when those who publish books describe how different it feels to write one. "Writing a book is a constant series of exposures," said Jacqueline Deval, director of publicity for William Morrow and author of the novel *Reckless Appetites*. Despite her intimate acquaintance with the publishing process, Deval was unprepared for the sense of vulnerability she experienced as a writer, "from handing over the finished manuscript to having strangers read it to galleys going out to more strangers to being in front of an audience. When the reviews appear, people from the past appear, so you're really out there in the world. It's also getting calls from strangers at home. That's alarming, a kind of exposure you can't control."

As author-editors discover, all the other anxieties—the many courage points of the writing process—are merely stretching exercises for the big one: feeling *exposed* (in every sense of the word).

3

Will Everyone See Through Me?

> Literature: proclaiming in front of
> everyone what one is careful to conceal
> from one's immediate circle.
> —*Jean Rostand*

*S*hortly after *The Great Santini* was published, Pat Conroy and I took part in an authors' program in Charlotte, North Carolina. Conroy starred his father in his novel-memoir and gave the rest of his family supporting roles. To this reader, *The Great Santini*'s portraits are sharp, true, and loving. Those portrayed had a different perspective. According to Pat, his father—whom he'd immortalized as the tyrannical Colonel "Bull" Meecham—called him after reading each chapter to ask in a choked voice why he hated him so much. Pat's mother stopped speaking to him altogether. In person, Pat Conroy was as genial as a pal from high school. I admired his guts in writing so candidly about himself and his family. Only later did I learn the rest of the story.

After he finished reading his son's novel, Don Conroy disappeared for three days. At one point he showed up in Atlanta's Old New York Book Shop to ask its owner—a close friend of Pat's—"Why is he doing this shit to me?" Pat's mother, Peg, was horrified by her son's retelling of their family's secrets. He was off in Atlanta. She still lived in Beaufort, South Carolina, where much of *The Great Santini* is set. Don's relatives shunned Pat. Peg's devoutly Christian relatives handed out pamphlets at his book signings urging customers not to buy *The Great Santini*. They wanted nothing more to do with him. Neither did Peg, at least until she divorced her husband of thirty-three years in *The Great Santini*'s aftermath. Pat himself went into therapy soon after the book appeared. On balance, he said, the whole Conroy clan reacted to his novel about them by having "a collective nervous breakdown."

Although seldom this extreme, such episodes are not uncommon in the lives of writers. Most adults enjoy the privilege of keeping their private lives private. Writers forgo that privilege. One author I know compared writing novels to dancing naked on a table. (She'd done both.) Other writers have their own metaphors for feeling exposed. Most involve some state of undress. "A person who publishes a book willfully appears before the populace with his pants down," said Edna St. Vincent Millay. E. B. White thought essay writing called for taking off one's trousers without showing one's genitals. When his letters were about to be published, however, White said he felt like a nudist with only bare skin between him and the reading public.

That Naked Feeling

That's about how writers feel in general. Those who put words on paper for public consumption live in fear that whoever reads their words will see right through them. At the very least, readers will discover what they themselves have suspected all along: that they're faking it. John Kenneth Galbraith said he never sat down to write without thinking to himself, "You'll be found out."

Writers don't just torture themselves with questions like "Can I pull it off?" and "Am I any good?" They also ask: "Will I be exposed as an impostor who set out to write *War and Peace* and ended up with *Dick and Jane*?" "Will readers laugh at my pathetic efforts?" "Will they look deep inside me and see nothing there?"

Such doubts growl with particular ferocity on the eve of book publication. Just before her best-selling first novel, *The Midwife*, was published, Gay Courter wrote me a letter about the evolution of her fears. In it she said:

> First, I was afraid it "would never sell," and I was "wasting my time," and everyone would know I wasted three years on the typical stupid N.J. housewife's ambition to "write the great American novel." Now I'm afraid that the book is going to sell and a) everyone will find out I'm a lousy writer; and b) everyone's going to see my innermost self through the book and know things I don't want them to know. The latter is already a problem as people who've read the manuscript ask if sex is really like that for me or what charac-

ter my husband is or do I really feel that way about my mother.

Every word we write for publication subjects us to scrutiny. The root of the term *publication*, after all, is *public*; those who read and judge a writer's work. This includes not only strangers but relatives, coworkers, neighbors, and perhaps the meter reader. What are they going to think when they read our writing? Not just about its quality but about its author? What will people discover about us that we'd rather they didn't know?

Such questions put writers in a bind. To write well, they must write honestly; not in the literal but in the emotional sense. Readers enjoy a *poseur* on the page about as much as they do in person. To touch their readers' feelings, writers must first improve reception of their own, then set up loudspeakers so that others can listen in. Doing this creates potential problems that transcend chagrin. Emotionally candid writing can jeopardize important relationships. Any ongoing relationship is based on some discretion. Writing demands revelation. Reconciling this conflict puts writers in a literary-human bind: wanting to be open yet not wanting to offend those they care about. This is a fundamental courage point.

One of the more courageous pieces of student writing I've read described without inhibition what it was like to care for a mother with Alzheimer's disease. This essay reported the usual—the author's frustration at mothering a parent who behaved like an infant, the agony of not being recognized by that parent—and the unusual, such as lighting a backyard path to lead her mother home when she wandered. The most poignant section, however—painful and funny at once—described how the writer's mother regularly attempted to crawl into bed with her son-in-law, making lascivious comments as she did.

What made this piece of work so unique was its scrupulous honesty in depicting a primary relationship. More often, we pull the shades in this area, to the detriment of our writing. In her book *If You Want to Write*, Brenda Ueland described a typical self-censoring student in one of her writing workshops. First this student considered how she might portray a close relative. The traits that came to mind were not altogether flattering. This alarmed her. "My goodness, how could I ever have such a mean thought about Auntie Mae!" she wondered. Instead the student wrote, "She was just a dear, old lady with a roguish twinkle in her eyes." Observed Ueland: "Not from the true self and so no good."

Writers who overprotect themselves and others produce pallid results. Their words are guarded, artificial; intended to make them look more agreeable than they feel. "My writing persona is much nicer than I am," a colleague once told me. "He's a much more solid person." This is probably true of most authors. But the results pose a problem. Few of us—writers and readers alike—*feel* nice inside. That's why pleasant words forge such a weak bond between writer and reader. They lack authenticity. Philip Roth said he found niceness even more deadly in writers than he did in people generally. Their ingratiating words sit limply on the page. Candid ones stand up straight and demand our attention. This is not just because we all love gossip but because such words sound more genuine. They come from deeper within.

So one should just write with candor and hang the consequences, right? That's what many advise. Annie Dillard said you should write as if you're dying. Nadine Gordimer went farther. She argued that you should write as if you were already dead and it no longer mattered what anyone said about you. But it's not always that simple, is it? At least not for those who have ties to others they'd like to preserve. Aspiring writers are routinely told to write about what they know. This usually boils down to *who* they know: family, relatives, friends. Portraying such people with candor risks wounding and betraying them. Even writers who stick to their own inner life may horrify those to whom they're close ("I had no idea you felt that way!"). Yet these are the risks they must take to write well. Frederick Busch said he considered his very life to be at stake when writing novels because his characters incorporate "aspects of, reflections of, extensions of, meditations upon, the people I hold dear." As a result, said Busch, "the moments, memories, and emotions of it that I cherish— the people, therefore, whose presence in it makes me want to keep experiencing my life—all are at risk when I work."

Rita Dove has often mined her life as a wife and mother for her poetry. The poems that resulted have uncommon power. But even though Dove thinks it's absolutely necessary to read them aloud—to get secrets out in the open— doing so has taken a steely nerve. Six years before she became poet laureate of the United States, Dove wrote a poem that is based on a bath she took with her young daughter:

My daughter spreads her legs
to find her vagina:
hairless, this mistaken
bit of nomenclature
is what a stranger cannot touch
without her yelling. She demands
to see mine and momentarily
we're a lopsided star
among the spilled toys,
my prodigious scallops
exposed to her neat cameo.

And yet the same glazed
tunnel, layered sequences.
She is three; that makes this
innocent. *We're pink!*
she shrieks, and bounds off.

Every month she wants
to know where it hurts
and what the wrinkled string means
between my legs. *This is good blood*
I say, but that's wrong, too.
How to tell her that it's what makes us—
black mother, cream child.
That we're in the pink
and the pink's in us.

    What gives this poem such power is its dead-on honesty.
Any mother could imagine having this conversation with a
daughter and making these observations about the conversation—if she dared. Dove dared.

No wonder writers are so anxious. They're playing for the highest stakes: pride, reputation, love, commitment. Those who embark on the writer's journey face a cruel choice. Shall they paddle their kayak into rushing rapids by writing openly about what concerns them most? Or should they write more guardedly about less vital topics and stick to canoeing on calm lakes? Bold writers run the risk not only that readers in general will see right through them but that readers they care about will see them for who they are and walk away. Authors always feel in danger of being abandoned by loved ones. This is a potent fear. Yet it's as inevitable as writer's cramp when we presume to write words for others to read.

Censors in Chief

I recently watched a successful young author waiting to speak to an overflow crowd at a Dayton, Ohio, bookstore. This book—a first novel—had been reviewed favorably in prominent media. Its author had just returned from making publicity appearances in New York. "I'm glad I did New York before this," she whispered nervously to a friend. "As kind of a warm-up."

"That's funny," laughed the friend, "considering New York a warm-up for Dayton."

"But I didn't know anyone in New York," explained the writer as she surveyed the crowd. "Here I see lots of familiar faces. There's my mother, my grandmother, my sister. Oh, God."

Comedians say the hardest audiences are those that include familiar faces. Their worst-case scenario is of having a relative watch them perform. For a parent to be present is an utter calamity. Writers plead their case before this court every day. Any time they publish, authors put their fate in the hands of a jury comprising not only anonymous readers but colleagues, spouses, parents, children, and their Aunt Emily in Springfield.

When we assess what's inhibiting our writing, a good place to start is the opinion of those to whom we're tied. William Zinsser recalled that when he began writing a memoir, "I was half paralyzed by the awareness that my parents and my sisters were looking over my shoulder, if not actually perched there, and would read whatever version of their life came out of my typewriter. . . . Since then, reading the memoirs of other writers, I've always wondered how many passengers were along on the ride, subtly altering the ride." In some cases such passengers don't just alter the ride but bring it to a screeching halt. After interviewing me about one of my books, a television reporter confided that he had a novel in the works. Except he hadn't worked on it in a while. In fact it was buried in a desk drawer at home. Why didn't he complete his novel? I asked. Because he'd made the mistake of telling his mother about it, the reporter explained. After that she kept asking to see his work-in-progress. He tried to put her off by explaining that it was half-baked; meaningless. Why not let her judge that, said his mother. Since then she'd became an unwelcome presence at her son's writing sessions. Those sessions grew farther and farther apart. Then they stopped altogether. That was why his unfinished novel sat in a desk drawer.

Anxiety about reactions by others can cripple a writer. When expressed at all, this fear is usually articulated as, "What will people think of me when they read what I've written?" But it's not "people" we're most scared of. It's specific individuals. The opinion of fuzzy thousands (or millions) of readers isn't what inhibits us most as we ponder our choice of words. Rather it's the frown on a few faces that come clearly into focus: the typist, the guys at work, our mate, our kids. "I didn't mind the world knowing about my life," said actress Susan Strasberg after examining that life with brutal candor in *Bittersweet*, "but I wasn't sure I wanted my daughter to know."

I often ask writing students to picture privately the person whose response to their writing concerns them the most. Usually it's a spouse or parent. Sometimes it's another relative, a friend, or an old teacher. It could be an admired colleague or one they don't like but find intimidating. Whoever's opinion worries us the most is our "censor in chief." That person can feel like a scowling Torquemada scrutinizing every word we write. Neutralizing our fear of his reaction may not be possible. But imagining how we'll deal with him helps. Simply identifying our censor in chief can be a revelation. We don't always realize how much he directs our productions. And if we can temper our fear of a censor in chief's opinion, dealing with the reaction of anyone else is a piece of cake by comparison.

When she was alive, my mother censored me most (rather, I censored myself as I imagined her reading my writing). Although I'm not proud to say it, I became a better writer after she died. I've become better still since my father joined her. Among other things, I could only consider writing about my mother with any candor once her husband was no longer around to read what I had to say about his wife. Others have had similar experiences. After his parents died, John Fowles rewrote *The Magus*, polishing his prose and punching up the erotic scenes. He'd felt unable to do this sooner, Fowles explained, because of what he called "that number one horror for any writer—the dear them, your mum and dad."

Parents are the most ubiquitous censors in chief for writers at every level. Allen Ginsberg said he wrote "Howl" without intending to publish it because "I wouldn't want my daddy to see what was in there." Erica Jong could only write *Fear of Flying* because she was sure it would never be published. When that proved to be wrong, Jong was so anxious about her family's reaction to her raunchy novel that she considered withdrawing it from publication. Early in his career, author-editor Gordon Lish did just that. Lish said he bought back printer's plates of an autobiographical first novel after it was set in type because he wasn't prepared to accept the consequences of having his family read that novel. "I don't see how you can write fiction honestly and ably without interfering with serious relationships," concluded Lish.

Spilling the Beans

Playwright A. R. Gurney has spent much of his career interfering with serious relationships. Gurney's plays are based not just on his own life but on those of his family. This has exacted a stiff personal and professional price. After it opened in 1970, Gurney rewrote parts of *Scenes from American Life* to appease his mother and father (who had seen a script and didn't like what they saw). Despite this self-censorship, Gurney's parents found it excruciating to sit with friends and watch their son's depiction of them when *Scenes* opened in Buffalo. His realtor father subjected him to a tight-lipped silence for a long time afterward. "He felt that my writing . . . had gotten too close to home," explained the playwright. "He thought it was a violation of the family's privacy."

How did Gurney deal with this trauma? He wrote a play about it. Gurney's 1989 hit *The Cocktail Hour* portrays a fortysomething playwright named John who's come home to ask his family's permission to produce a play about them. John's father refuses. He offers his son $20,000 not to stage the play. "I don't want people laughing at me," explains the father, "or critics commenting about me, or the few friends I have left commiserating with me." After his father storms off, John's mother, Ann, says, "He's scared you'll spill the beans."

JOHN: The beans?

ANN: The beans.

JOHN: What beans?

ANN: Oh, John, face it. Everyone's got beans to spill. And, knowing you, you'll find a way to spill ours. . . .

JOHN: Family feelings, family feelings! The story of my life! The bane of my existence! Family feelings. Dear Mother, dear Pop. May I have permission to cross the street? May I have permission to buy a car? Would you mind very much if I screwed my girl?

ANN: Now that's enough of that, please.

JOHN: Well, it's true! Family feelings. May I have your approval to put on a play? Oh God, why did I come here? Why did I bother? Most playwrights dish out the most brutal diatribes against their parents, who sit proudly in the front row and applaud every insult that comes along. Me? Finally—after fifteen years of beating around the bush—I come up with something which is—all right, maybe a little on the nose, maybe a little frank, maybe a little satiric at times—but still clearly infused with warmth, respect, and an abiding affection, and what happens? I'm being censored, banned, bribed not to produce.

Although Gurney's father was no longer alive when *The Cocktail Hour* was produced, the playwright honored his mother's request not to let it be staged in their native Buffalo.

Like A. R. Gurney, many writers have discovered that the danger family members pose to a writer is not just hypothetical:

· Peter Taylor's father threatened him with physical mayhem because a story of his in *The New Yorker* incorporates an incident from the life of his great-aunt.

· Paul Hemphill's mother and sister toured Birmingham, Alabama, buying up every available copy of the Sunday *New York Times* with Paul's article about his hard-drinking father in its magazine, then used them to fuel a bonfire in their backyard.

· After Raymond Carver's mother finished reading a collection of her son's short stories—some of whose characters were based on her and other members of their family—she threw it to the floor. "It hurt," said Mrs. Carver of this experience, "and then it made me mad."

· Undismayed by his experience with *The Great Santini*, Pat Conroy based his next novel, *The Lords of Discipline*, on the experiences of himself and classmates at the Citadel, then focused *The Prince of Tides* on a troubled poet much like his sister, Carol Conroy. Carol—who'd warned Pat not to write about her—stopped speaking to him.

Any writer who depicts another person in a recognizable way is in jeopardy. Whether that depiction is positive, negative, or both doesn't necessarily matter. One can write an entire profile that portrays its subject as a loving parent, upstanding citizen, tops in his field, and a hell of a good softball player who has a mole on his left earlobe. Invariably that person will moan, "Did you have to mention the mole?" It's easy to dismiss such reactions as hypersensitive. Writers typically rationalize their subjects' outrage by saying that just as no one likes how he sounds on tape, no one likes how he looks on paper. But that's too simple, and self-serving. When our life is depicted by someone else, we have cause to feel misrepresented. This isn't necessarily because the writer's facts are wrong but because they're incomplete. She decided what the world should know about us, selecting elements from our life that served *her* purpose, not ours. That puts the writer in a very powerful position. Her word is the last word (literarily speaking) on the subject of us. When Gail Godwin's sister recognized elements of her life in a novel written by her sibling she complained, "I don't like being frozen in print for the rest of my life, forever wearing those silly panties and short skirts; and I'm *not* big like that, she's made me into some sort of Amazon-freak."

No one has considered the writer's right to requisition material from the life of others at greater length than has Philip Roth. After the firestorm he created by mining his upbringing in *Portnoy's Complaint*, Roth made the conflict between loyalty to art and to others an ongoing theme in several novels featuring the Rothlike writer Nathan Zuckerman. These novels are filled with characters who chastise Zuckerman for selfishly exploiting their lives to his own literary ends. Henry Zuckerman accuses his brother of hastening their father's death by writing a mocking family saga much like *Portnoy's Complaint*. In *The Counterlife*, Henry calls this "murdering their parents under the guise of art." During the same novel, he reflects that "all the blood relatives of an articulate artist are in a very strange bind, not only because they find that they are 'material,' but because their own material is always articulated for them by someone else who, in his voracious, voyeuristic using-up of all their lives, gets there first but doesn't always get it right."

In *The Anatomy Lesson*, Roth wrote of Henry's wife, Carol:

> She always pretended when he [Zuckerman] was around to know nothing, to have read nothing, to have no thoughts on any subject; if he was in the same room, she wouldn't even dare to recount an anecdote, though Zuckerman often heard from his mother how "thoroughly delightful" she could be when she and Henry entertained the family. But Carol herself, in order to reveal nothing he could criticize or ridicule, revealed to him nothing at all. All he knew for sure about Carol was that she didn't want to wind up in a book.

In these and many other passages Roth shows an acute awareness of the suspicion and resentment of those who might become grist for a novelist's quill. Nonetheless, Roth's own attitude was—unequivocally—that whatever happens to the writer is fair game, *material*. Even the rage of family members can be a source of literary energy. When radio interviewer Susan Stamberg told Roth about a writer whose mother had sued him, Roth's said, "That's a wonderful story! He should write that story!"

"Yeah, maybe he will," replied Stamberg, "—if he can recover from the trauma of his mother having sued him."

Retorted Roth: "Yes, well, if he can't recover, then he oughtn't to be a writer. Those scruples only get in his way. It's a very unscrupulous profession, you know."

Scalawags and Spies

Many of Roth's colleagues agree. They don't just accept betraying others as an unfortunate by-product of writing but seem to positively relish being devious scalawags. There's an unmistakable tone of hubris as such writers 'fess up to their lack of scruples.

> I'm basically a treacherous person with no sense of loyalty. I'd write openly about my sainted mother's sex life for art.
>
> —*Susan Braudy*

. . . . .

> Is it true that writers are pillagers of privacy? Yes. And it is also true that others get hurt along the way. But what are a few hurt feelings along the fiction trail?
>
> —*Annie Roiphe*

. . . . .

> Isn't disloyalty as much the writer's virtue as loyalty is the soldier's?
>
> —*Graham Greene*

Writers rarely discuss the sense of moral cowardice to which they're susceptible; of being willing to write things about others that they could never say to their faces. Writers by definition talk behind other people's backs. Much of their work is refined gossip. They are snoopers, eavesdroppers.

I once assigned a group of college students to portray someone they didn't know, providing enough detail to bring that person to life. During lunch, one of my students sat down next to me. "What exactly did you mean by the assignment?" she asked. Rather than try to explain, I looked around the cafeteria. Two tables away a sociology professor chatted with a student. "Let's watch him," I said. Above the tabletop this man was a picture of ease. He conversed casually with the student, made good eye contact, and kept his hands folded calmly. Beneath the table, another drama was being played out. There the teacher tapped his toes, jiggled his knees, and curled his legs around each other like two boa constrictors wrestling. This man was leading a double life. I pointed that out to my student. Could she capture this scene in words?

The girl blushed a deep crimson. "I couldn't," she murmured.

"Why not?" I asked.

"I'd feel like a spy."

Exactly. That's how writers often feel. When it comes to their own family and friends, writers can feel like double agents: pretending to be loyal comrades even as they secretly plot to betray them in print. Tobias Wolff once observed with a chuckle that although Raymond Carver was the most sympathetic listener to his friends' problems, "later he would be absolutely ruthless about using anything he heard."

Cold Hearts, Hot Words

It's hard for a writer not to feel like a moral cipher; someone likely to use any person, reveal any secret, exploit any episode in the quest for "material." Joan Didion's observation that "writers are always selling somebody out" struck a painful note of recognition among her colleagues. The reason Didion's comment gets repeated so often by other writers is that they know how true it is. At an extreme, they look within and see the "splinter of ice" that Graham Greene thought was impaled in every writer's heart. Yet writers know that a cold heart is only effective when applied to hot words. The work they do calls on them to convey strong feelings with the cool detachment of a neurosurgeon operating on a brain. This leads to a bifurcated life: one lived and observed simultaneously. "All that he sees," said Guy de Maupassant of the writer, "his joys, his pleasures, his suffering, his despair, all instantaneously become objects of observation. . . . He has not a spark of enthusiasm, not a cry, not a kiss that is spontaneous, not one instantaneous action done merely because it must be done, unconsciously, without understanding, without writing it down afterwards. He says to himself as he leaves the cemetery where he has left the being he loved most in the world, 'it is curious what I felt . . .' "

This risk is not just hypothetical. Arnold Bennett insisted that a deathbed scene in one of his novels could not be faulted for its verisimilitude. He took infinite pains with this scene, explained Bennett: "All the time my father was dying, I was at the bedside making copious notes."

This raises an important question every writer must answer. Are there limits to what, and who, can be incorporated in their work? Many say there aren't, or at least shouldn't be. When Willa Cather based a short story on the disfigurement of a friend, a group of mutual friends pleaded with her not to publish this story. They were concerned that it might devastate the woman on whom it was based and even lead to her suicide (as in the story itself). Cather's response was, "My art is more important than my friend."

How do writers deal with such a self-portrait? The most common approach is to say there's no alternative. In this school of thought, the reactions of others are no concern to a *real* artist. "A writer's only responsibility is to his art," said William Faulkner. "He will be completely ruthless if he is a good one. He has a dream. It anguishes him so much he must get rid of it. He has no peace until then. Everything goes by the board: honor, pride, decency, security, happiness—all to get his book written. If a writer has to rob his mother, he will not hesitate: the 'Ode on a Grecian Urn' is worth any number of old ladies."

One hesitates to argue with Faulkner about artistic integrity, but let's do so anyway, just for the sake of argument. The annals of literary history are littered with those—including Faulkner—who ignored families, betrayed friends, and suffered profound despair in pursuit of their grail. One reason so many good writers have such tattered personal lives is that they write as if they had no one to protect. Lucky for readers; not so lucky for writers. Unluckiest of all are such author's families. The writer is also a human being. Creating a successful life is at least as worthy a goal as writing well (and considerably more difficult). Robert Lowell thought it was harder to be a good man than a great poet. After endorsing this observation, Stephen Spender added, "The great poet or writer is faced by the dilemma that in order to accomplish his art he must be a selfish person. Think how James Joyce, for example, sacrificed his family."

There are two schools of thought on the writer's responsibility to a spouse and children. Joan Didion spoke for one school when she said she was a writer first, wife and mother second. Some writers go farther. They consider family not just a passive but an active impediment to art. In the words of Cyril Connolly, "There is no more somber enemy of good art than the pram in the hall." Ken Kesey articulated the other position when he explained his extended disappearance from the literary scene by saying he could write forever but had only a short time to raise his children. "I thought raising a family was a lot more important than writing," said Kesey.

Between those extremes, most writers muddle through, trying to write their best without betraying those they love, and hoping to be humane without limiting their output to homilies. It may be true that writers shouldn't concern themselves with what "people" might think of them. Family and friends are another matter. Most writers realize they could write more openly by ignoring the sensibilities of those to whom they're tied. It's just not worth the price. Eugene O'Neill left instructions that *Long Day's Journey into Night*, which drew on his family in such harrowing detail, should not be published until twenty-five years after his parents died (his widow did so anyway, three years after their death). William Humphrey—who deeply offended his mother with the autobiographical novel *Farther Off from Heaven*—wouldn't publish a short story based on old acquaintances until they were dead. Norman Mailer said he drew the line at putting his wife in his work. Many a writer has written boldly about parents, siblings, and relatives. Few are so blithe about portraying their own children.

Between the poles of *write and be damned!* and *don't write at all* (you might hurt someone), all writers must find their point of moral, emotional, and literary integrity. How they resolve the conflict between writing well and being humane determines not only what type of writers they become but what type of people. A Faulkner, a Cather, or a Carver forge ahead regardless. One admires their valor and their artistic integrity (to say nothing of their writing). Other authors have chosen to be more circumspect. As a young writer, memoirist Ned Rorem never realized that he might hurt friends with his literary candor. In time they disabused him. As a result, said Rorem, "I've now come to value discretion, even to claim it among virtues far higher than mere truth."

Within the extremes of candor and discretion, all writers must go where their moral compass takes them. This subject demands reflection. To brush it aside as a nonissue, or one with an obvious answer, is no solution.

Beyond "Write and Be Damned!"

Selling others out versus writing pallid prose are not the only alternatives for a writer. Important Others can be tended to before, during, and after the writing process. Rita Dove regularly asked her daughter if she was embarrassed by her mother reading aloud the poem about them comparing vaginas. (Through the age of ten, Dove's daughter said she wasn't.) Before he published *Another Roadside Attraction*, Tom Robbins wrote his mother a long letter preparing her for what she was about to read. "I spent almost as much time on that letter as I did on the book," said Robbins. Isabel Allende reminded her friends regularly, "Beware: everything you say can be used against you." Even when she did want to use a friend's experience in a novel, Allende first asked permission. "To me," she explained, "a friend is more important than a character."

Like Allende, I try to let others know in advance when I'm drawing on their lives in my writing. That way, I'm not anxious about "what they're going to think" after a book or article of mine comes out that includes such material. I already know. Consulting others in this manner is risky. The hand of self-censorship can be very subtle as one imagines the reaction of those to be consulted. It's also none too accurate. A friend of mine gave her husband veto power over anything she wrote about him in a book of essays. He blue-penciled only three sentences, none of which were ones she thought would offend him, and left in every episode she was sure he'd object to.

Though unpredictable, this consultation process can also be liberating. Rarely does anyone object to my using material I ask about. And because they know I'll ask, family and friends are less likely to protect themselves when talking with me. Quite the contrary; many get remarkably quotable when they know I'm working on a book. Other writers have found the same reactions. Some friends get mad if you put them in your work; others get mad if you *don't*. "I've known a few men who were delighted at the possibility that I would write about them," said novelist Elizabeth Benedict. " 'Have I been around long enough to make it into a short story?' one asked."

A fear of others' reactions to our work often turns out to be greater in our own mind than in theirs. Also, the consequences of writing about others are not necessarily bad. Getting issues on the table via words in print may be a volatile form of family therapy, but it can be effective nonetheless. After *Fear of Flying* was published, Erica Jong's father opened up to her about his own erotic life. Allen Ginsberg ended up giving joint poetry readings with the father whose reaction to "Howl" so concerned him.

After writing an essay about my own father, I sent him a copy of the final draft. Afterward I could think of little other than how he might react. Although my essay was positive overall, and loving, it was not a total rave. We'd had problems, and I wrote about them. Three days after I sent him my essay, Dad called. In a trembling voice, with no preamble, he said, "Ralph, I love it." Dad said how touched and honored he felt that I'd written about him. Then he laughed and admitted he'd been dropping pearls for years in hopes I'd pick them up and put them on paper.

Other writers have had similar experiences with family members whose imagined reaction caused them so much anguish.

• *Newsweek*'s Michel Marriott wrote a magazine article describing his stormy relationship with a stern father. "There had been times when we had hurled hurtful words at each other like poison-tipped spears," wrote Marriott. But Marriott also wrote of his regard for his father, a factory worker in Louisville. He explained that this regard was due in part to "my empathy with his life and wounds as a proud

Black man dangling from a leafless tree of opportunities denied." Despite the mixed tone of his son's review, Marriott's father was thrilled. "You gave me hell, but you did so eloquently," he told his son. The senior Marriott even memorized parts of his son's essay and recited them for friends.

· Years after Paul Hemphill's mother and sister made a bonfire of the article he wrote about his father, Hemphill's father died. Going through his father's effects, Paul found a box in the basement filled with his own published work. In this box was a copy of the piece Paul wrote about him. Across the top was scrawled, "All true. All true."

· The title of Amy Tan's novel *The Joy Luck Club* was the actual name of a mah-jongg group to which her mother belonged. That novel drew liberally on elements of Daisy Tan's life. These included the fact that Daisy's own mother died of an opium overdose, that her first husband abused her and had affairs, and that she had to leave her children behind when fleeing to America. Yet Amy Tan's mother accepted with equanimity even those episodes that embarrassed her. Of her daughter's best-selling success, Daisy said, "Not bad for a girl who fought with Mom and did not become doctor."

· In response to his son's portrayal of him as a schoolteacher in *The Centaur*, John Updike's father said, "The kid caught me exactly." Like many authors, Updike found his parents were more serene about his writing than he had feared they'd be. "I find it's harder to shock my parents than I might have thought. No matter what you write, they're able to still love you completely as their son."

· Once the furor about his son's novel subsided, Don Conroy took to signing Christmas cards "The Great Santini" and driving a car with SANTINI license plates. When the movie made of his son's book received Oscar nominations, Don stormed into his son's apartment, saying, "Son, you and I were nominated for Academy Awards last night. Your mother didn't get crap." At times he showed up at Pat's book signings to add his own signature. When Barbra Streisand started filming *The Prince of Tides*, Pat presented her with a copy of *The Great Santini* inscribed at length by his father. (Lest this sound too much like a Hollywood ending, Pat and Don Conroy have continued to duel furiously in the press.)

Seven years after *Is There Life After High School?* was published, I attended my twentieth class reunion. This was not an easy task. Because so many classmates had either read my book or seen me discuss it on television, I knew they realized that I'd portrayed our time together in less than favorable terms. I was convinced that at least one of them would be waiting inside the door of the American Legion hall to hit me in the nose.

To my surprise, not only did no classmate try to hit me (I'm still not convinced that no one wanted to) but those who approached me seemed more curious than offended by what I'd written. A couple confided that their reactions to our high school days were much like mine. The biggest surprise of all, however, was my own feeling of calm as the evening wore on. Having vented my spleen on the page, I felt no need to repeat myself. Nor did I spend the reunion seething with unexpressed anger. It had all been expressed. What I did feel was free to indulge in fond feelings for my classmates, feelings that turned out to be stronger than I realized. After beginning the evening in a state of near panic, I left the reunion feeling more serene than I'd felt in years.

The issue of conscripting others into the ranks of our writing is complicated. However one approaches it takes nerve: to tell the truth and take the consequences, or to protect others and risk mediocrity. There is no easy resolution of this dilemma. But facing the predicament squarely is better than avoiding it. In the process, writers usually find they can draw more openly on their lives than they thought was possible. One reason is the discovery that much of what they assumed to be anxiety about the opinions of others turns out to be anxiety about their own opinion of themselves.

$\overset{4}{\underline{}}$

The Devil in the Inkstand

> Everyone has talent. What is rare
> is the courage to follow that talent
> to the dark place where it leads.
> —*Erica Jong*

*W*hen she started writing fiction, Sherri Szeman decided not to draw on her own life. "I'm not interesting enough," explained Szeman. That sounded prudent. Yet her first novel was anything but prudent. A Gentile in her late thirties, Szeman did original research about the Holocaust—including interviews with survivors—to write *The Kommandant's Mistress*. This novel portrays a concentration camp commander and the Jewish inmate he forces to become his concubine. Szeman's book is filled with brutality, murder, and violent sex. Writing it subjected the author to multiple risks: of exploiting her subject, portraying horror with candor, and making a Nazi officer understandable (if not sympathetic). Szeman's unsparing depiction of the commandant's sadomasochistic relationship with his mistress provides what the *New Yorker* called "a guilty, addictive thrill."

By making her narrative skip around in time, Szeman spares readers unrelieved horror. The author wasn't so fortunate. Even though her novel is not about herself, directly, Szeman had to dig deep inside to discover the emotional wellsprings from which to work, then report honestly what she'd discovered. *The Kommandant's Mistress* includes horrifying scenes of torture, of a young boy finding his mother hanging in an attic, and of the novel's heroine being taken from her parents (who proceed to the gas ovens) after they arrive at the concentration camp. These were not easy passages to write. One of the most demanding scenes isn't about the death camp itself but is a postwar sequence in which the heroine's husband leaves her. This scene cut close enough to Szeman's own bones that she couldn't write it for weeks. The result of this harrowing process was a first novel of such power that it received nearly unanimous praise from reviewers and readers. Concentration camp survivors who read *The Kommandant's Mistress* had trouble believing that any nonsurvivor could have written this book, let alone a young Gentile who had spent her entire life in southwestern Ohio. Szeman's success was due in part to her research but even more to her willingness to go to dark inner places most of us avoid.

Writing about others and risking their wrath takes one type of courage. Writing from within—as Szeman did—takes another. Unlike the more conscious fear of others, anxiety about our inner world tends to be repressed. It often shows up in disguise. The most common disguise is fear of *them, their* opinion of us, when it's actually our own opinion of ourselves that we're worried about. In psychological terms, much of our fear about the reaction of others is a projection of our own anxieties.

The Secret Self

We all have secrets locked tightly in an inner safe. Writers must unlock that safe and risk letting its contents creep onto the page. "A book is the writer's secret life," said Faulkner, "the dark twin of a man." Exposing that life takes courage. Who among us has the valor to casually let her secret self escape from the lockbox in her head, dash through her fingers onto paper, then make its way to a publisher and bookstore, only to end up on coffee tables around the country so readers can have a look?

When making public appearances, I often meet aspiring writers. Many tell me that they, too, hope to publish. Although I try to encourage them all, I know that few will. Among other reasons, once they realize the psychological demands that writing places on them, other pursuits will begin to look more appealing. Aspiring writers are often driven to write because there are things deep inside them they want to get out. But after they peer deeply within, few remain sure that they want anyone else to know the most interesting things they see.

"Writing exposes your innermost thoughts and is embarrassing," explained Jonellen Heckler, the author of five novels. Nearly two decades ago, Heckler approached me after a speech to say that she, too, hoped to publish someday. As usual, I made some vague, reassuring comments, never expecting to see her name in print. I was wrong. Within a couple of years Heckler's byline began to appear on short stories in women's magazines. Then her first novel—*Safe-keeping*—was published, followed by four more. Heckler's second novel, *A Fragile Peace*, portrays a family caught in the grips of an alcoholic father much like her own. Needless to say, this was not an easy book to write. But *A Fragile Peace* wasn't the book Heckler found most demanding. *Safekeeping*—which depicts an extramarital love affair—was harder. A happily married wife and mother, Heckler didn't find it easy to write about illicit lovemaking. Letting others know that she had such wanton thoughts didn't concern the novelist as much as her own fear that portraying an affair was tantamount to having one. "I had to come to terms with the fact that writing about something was not the moral equivalent of doing it," said Heckler. "I would not commit adultery, but I wanted to write a whole book about an affair. I know it sounds simpleminded, but I actually had to have a conversation with myself about this in the beginning, convincing myself that it was all right to depict this affair."

Any writing exposes writers to judgment about the quality of their work and their thought. The closer they get to painful personal truths, the more fear mounts—not just about what they might reveal but about what they might *discover* should they venture too deeply inside. To write well, however, that's exactly where we must venture. Melville admired most the writers he called "divers," those who dared to plunge deep inside and report what they found. Frederick Busch thought this need for inner exploration was what made novel-writing so daring. "You go to dark places so that you can get there, steal the trophy and get out," said Busch. "That is more important than to be psychologically safe."

We all keep thoughts to ourselves in a zone of privacy. The bigger that zone, the worse our writing. A rich vein of material usually hides within our protected self. An emotional mother lode lies buried in the deepest caverns. Compelling writing is a result of strong feelings with a sharp edge. The feelings that produce such writing aren't necessarily ones we want to admit harboring. It takes courage not just to expose such feelings to others but to reveal them to ourselves.

"I am smoking almost two packs a day," wrote a forty-six-year-old unemployed executive in an essay about his status. "I try not to drink before 5 o'clock."

> The other day I encountered the man who fired me. He is an affable, bright man, and on the eve of retirement. Many months ago he told me I had outlived my usefulness, and he wished me well. The other day he said he knew what I had been going through. When I said he didn't, he looked just a little startled. He does not, never did, like to be contradicted. But I knew he had never been without work. I told him that physically, fiscally, and spiritually I and all members of my family had been wiped out. Then he asked why I was having such trouble finding a new job.
>
> The easiest, possibly even the only truthful answer would have been this: "No one wants me." That is the way I feel, of course. (Paranoia. Depression. I used to think they were modern conveniences that only others could afford.) But I told him what I know: My age, sex, and salary needs work against me. So, of course, does the shortage of jobs. Then he turned to talk with another passer-by; he meant well, though.

Aspiring writers are typically advised to speak from the heart. Just relax and be yourself, they're told. Relax? How can I relax when I'm putting bleeding tissue on display to be voted up or down (down, most likely)? Let's go farther. Suppose I don't know who I am and am scared to find out. I once asked a reticent student in his forties why he was afraid to write what he felt. "I'm not afraid to *write* what I feel," this man replied. "I'm afraid to *feel* what I feel."

Writers have no alternative. Any writing that calls on the reader's feelings must first call on the author's. "No tears in the writer, no tears in the reader," said Robert Frost. Writers can use devices—comic relief and the like—to go easy on readers. But they can't go easy on themselves. While writing, they must subject themselves to the full range of feelings they discover, even those from which they protect the reader. They must have the courage to go where their minds wander, and be stalwart in facing down inner censors. Writers must also learn to be forgiving of themselves if everything they discover along the way isn't to their liking.

I'm often asked why I write so often about "negative" subjects: tensions between fathers and sons, adolescent angst, time pressure. My answer is that exploring such topics on paper helps me get rid of them. Writing can be wonderful therapy, and cheap at the price. At the very least, you eventually get bored by thinking about anxious topics and want to move on.

Setting off on a literary journey of self-exploration needn't be uninviting. Rita Dove has said she finds composing poems a first-rate way to explore her guilts, fears, and joys, in the process "calling up emotions that I don't quite have a handle on and, by writing about them, understand them a little better." Like Dove, some welcome the opportunity to get to know themselves better by writing.

John Cheever said writing fiction was the best means he'd found to make sense of his life. John Updike called fiction writing "the subtlest instrument for self-examination and self-display that mankind has invented yet."

Honest Fiction

Many start writing fiction as a dodge, thinking it will provide a good hideout from themselves. Yet those who write stories and novels to escape from themselves invariably discover that this is who they stumble over at every turn. Even though novelists and short story writers ostensibly deal in fantasy, they are the most self-exposed authors of all. Writers of nonfiction can be judged on their ability to marshal facts coherently and gracefully. Poets can hide behind elegant words, powerful metaphors, and seductive rhythms. Fiction writers are judged by the emotional authenticity of their work. To create authentic feelings in their characters, they must first call up their own.

The most famous scene in Pat Conroy's *The Great Santini* portrays a one-on-one basketball game that Marine Colonel "Bull" Meecham loses to his eighteen-year-old son, Ben. Meecham is not a graceful loser. He demands they resume play, that Ben come back to guard him.

> "I'm not gonna guard you, Dad. I won," Ben said, his voice almost breaking. He could feel himself about to cry.
>
> Bull saw it too. "That's it, mama's boy. Start to cry. I want to see you cry," Bull roared, his voice at full volume, a voice of drill fields, a voice to be heard above the thunder of jet engines, a voice to

be heard above the din of battle. Bull took the basketball and threw it into Ben's forehead. Ben turned to walk into the house, but Bull followed him, matching his steps and throwing the basketball against his son's head at intervals of three steps. Bull kept chanting, "Cry, cry, cry," each time the ball ricocheted off his son's skull. Through the kitchen Ben marched, through the dining room, never putting his hands behind his head to protect himself, never trying to dodge the ball. Ben just walked and with all his powers of concentration rising to the surface of consciousness, of being alive, and of being son, Ben tried not to cry. That was all he wanted to derive from the experience, the knowledge that he had not cried.

Even though this incident didn't happen, Pat Conroy found that writing it forced him to confront long-repressed feelings about his abusive father. "The scene upset me badly," said Conroy. "I had created a boy named Ben Meecham and had given him my story. His loneliness, his unbearable solitude, almost killed me as I wrote about him. I simply could not bear the weight of what I was saying. We had hidden my father's betrayal so completely—no one knew outside the family. It started all the engines up for me, the engines people in therapy know about but I had no idea about."

One reason I've stuck to nonfiction is that fiction might lead me into dark caves I'm hesitant to explore. "Facts," oddly enough, can be easier to hide behind psychologically than so-called stories. Those who dare to write novels and short stories have always impressed me as writing's real heroes. This could just be an eyes-of-the-beholder phenomenon. Some novelists feel that nonfiction writers are the real Joans of Arc, exhorting the troops with straight talk while they cravenly feed to made-up characters lines that they're scared to say themselves. "Any essayist setting out on a frail apparatus of notings and jottings is a brave person," argued novelist Diane Johnson. "The novelist, afraid his ideas may be foolish, slyly puts them into the mouth of some other fool and reserves the right to disavow them."

Be that as it may, I still admire fiction writers' guts. Novelists and short story writers face the blank page without interview notes to consult. They must turn over rocks that conceal feelings most of us leave hidden. Postpublication comments have to be fielded ("Did your dad really bounce a basketball off your head?"). Even when readers are persuaded that an author used more imagination than reporting skills, the question remains, "How could you even *think* the things you wrote about?" The corollary to that question is, "I'm not sure how I feel about someone who has thoughts like that." Finally, critics assess novelists more on the quality of their art—which feels closer to the quick of the self—than on the quality of their research or even their ideas. "Maybe the nature of fiction is that, unlike reporting for the *New York Times*, it has to admit everything," said E. L. Doctorow, "—all aspects and forms of thought and behavior and feeling, no matter how awful they may be. Fiction has no borders; everything is open, you have a limitless possibility of knowing the truth."

The facts of the matter are less demanding to write about than the feelings. Literal truth doesn't demand as much from a writer as emotional truth. Before they can convey honest feeling to others, writers must be honest with themselves. This sounds simple but isn't. Ernest Hemingway thought one of the hardest tasks confronting writers was to determine their real feelings, not ones they were supposed to have. Hemingway tried. Not all writers do. "What I know about me I do not wish to admit," confessed Hemingway's friend, Janet Flanner. "So this knowledge is canceled because of its unpleasantness. This basic evasion probably disbalances all my possibilities of self-information."

Flanner spent half a century reporting from Paris for the *New Yorker* under the pseudonym Genêt. Doing so gave her the freedom to write with a sophisticated, omniscient voice foreign to her own. It also made her feel like an impostor. Even worse, after spending so much time in disguise producing literary trifles, Flanner felt unable to shift gears and write fiction of substance. Hiding behind a pseudonym, Flanner finally concluded, had allowed her to avoid the introspection and self-revelation that any serious writer must risk. Her inability to look within ultimately made Flanner feel like a cowardly failure. "She feared she had ignored her inner life," reported Flanner's biographer, Brenda Wineapple, "preferring to skate on the surfaces of things; having failed to seek 'news of' an 'inner soul' she feared she would never be able to create anything she truly respected." Flanner died at the age of eighty-six without having produced any fiction of the quality she'd dreamed of writing.

Peering into the Void

Unlike the more conscious fear of being revealed to others, the fear of being revealed to ourselves tends to be repressed.

By this I mean fear of the rage, violence, and unbridled lust that we might discover any time our fingers run riot across a page. Authors routinely find that what they write bears no relation to what they meant to write; that some gremlin begins dancing across their keyboard or pushing their pen around. "The devil himself gets into my inkstand," complained Nathaniel Hawthorne.

It takes courage to go where this gremlin beckons. In the process, some writers virtually black out. It's as if they'd been taken on board an alien spacecraft to write, then returned to their desks with no memory of where they'd been or what they'd done. While reading galleys of her novel *Delta Wedding*, Eudora Welty came upon a page of dialogue that she couldn't remember writing. Welty wondered if a typesetter had accidentally inserted this page. She called her editor to ask. Very gently—as if this had happened before—the editor read aloud from Welty's own manuscript the exact words she didn't recognize in her galleys.

Our best writing results from a partnership of the conscious and unconscious. The conscious mind imposes a needed discipline on its counterpart's spontaneity but is also the one most worried about appearances. The conscious mind is our censoring mind. To overcome writing anxiety, we must keep its appearance-consciousness from bullying us. Setting the unconscious free to battle its more inhibited mate is the best way to do this. Some can't. The prospect of letting their unconscious traipse about—unknown, uncontrolled, feral—is too disturbing. Others find the thought appealing. John Hersey said that when his work was going well, he entered something like a dream state. The fictional "voice" he acquired in this state was one he didn't control. Hersey wasn't sure exactly where it came from. He did know that its home base was not in his intellect. "I think a writer is on track when the door of his native and deeper intuitions is open," said Saul Bellow. "You write a sentence that doesn't come from that source and you can't build around it—it makes the page seem somehow false."

The farther writing strays from its deepest sources, the more sterile it becomes. Words skimmed from the surface grow tiresome. Subliminally the reader senses that the writer isn't saying what he most wants to say. He's protecting himself; being prudent. Writers realize this more consciously. One of the worst things they can say about a colleague is that he played it safe. They judge each other and themselves as much on courage and candor as on competence and craft. "The only writers I respect," said Henry Miller, "are those who have put themselves completely into their work. Not those who use their skillful hands to do something. This isn't writing, in my opinion. A man who can dash off a book, let's say, and say it's a good novel, a best seller, even of some value, but it isn't representative completely of him, of his personality, then there's something wrong there. This man is a fraud in a way, to me. All he put into his book was his skill. And that's nothing. I prefer a man who is unskillful, who is an awkward writer, but who has something to say, who is dealing himself one time on every page."

Style Is the Man, and Woman

In writing, as in life, however, "being yourself" is easier to propose than practice. The need to do so is a key source of writing anxiety. Being ourselves raises the stakes of rejection immeasurably. It's bad enough to present a stylized self to the reading public and have that self rejected. But at least then we can take comfort in the fact that it wasn't us, the real us, that was rebuffed. On the other hand, if we reach down deep to bring up the most honest words we can find and then get pasted, well . . .

It's no wonder so many writers struggle ingeniously to hide behind verbiage and poses. And no wonder apprentice writers spend so many years developing a style that apes someone else's: Hemingway, Woolf, Wolfe (both of them). Borrowing someone else's voice postpones the day when we must discover our own. Our risk of exposure is lessened because we've donned the mask of an established writer. It also makes for deadly writing. Just as Thomas Wolfe ruined a generation of novelists who reproduced Wolfe's wordiness without his intensity, Tom Wolfe today is imitated by legions of admirers who mimic his eccentric style but can't capture his voice because it isn't their own.

Here is a paragraph from a writer who spent too much time trying to be like Tom, too little developing a personal style to address the reader without affectation:

> Bob Dole didn't see the ball game. He was working. Probably hadn't seen a whole game since high school. He knew what he had to know about it. Like it, sure, as far as that went. Not too far. Might see a few pitches, in passing, on the console thing in his living room. TV, VCR, radio, all in one sort of console, right in front of the easy chair. Everything he needed, if

he was home. Wasn't home much. What would
he do there?

The originator of a distinctive voice wins applause for
her daring and singularity. Imitators work from a timidity
that mostly annoys. As editor of *The American Spectator*,
R. Emmett Tyrrell, Jr., has spent his career trying to resur-
rect the voice of H. L. Mencken. The results range from
tedious to ludicrous.

> There are in our time vast hosts of demi-
> educated believers. Inculcated with lofty notions
> at educational plants, these patheticoes enter the
> adult world full of self-righteousness, fear of
> modern life, and the desperate will to believe in
> their supercilious mountebanks. During the past
> decade their influence has profoundly flum-
> moxed American society, particularly our gov-
> ernment and our economy. Yet as conditions
> worsen, they holler all the more violently for
> more of the mountebanks' flimflam.

Readers read such derivative writing with an irritated
feeling: okay, okay, what do *you* have to say? Only when the
writer's own voice breaks through do they sit up and pay
attention. Readers are then also free to judge the writer as a
person; not as a ventriloquist's dummy mouthing someone
else's words. This prospect is daunting enough that many
writers—even gifted ones—never do develop their own
voice. Given the opportunity to understand themselves
better by writing, and share that understanding with readers, they choose instead to don a costume.

Compare the affectation of Tyrrell's inflated verbiage or that of the Wolfelike journalist with the simple eloquence of this poem by a homeless New Yorker named Randy:

> Living in the shadow of everything
> I bleed from self-inflicted wounds
> Never venturing out—tucked safely
>   away in the shadows . . .
> Violence is my constant companion
> Loneliness my only friend
> Hunger is my chief adviser
> I have willingly chosen this as a way of
>   not being with myself . . .
> My daily mission is to obliterate the
>   memories of where I come from
> Of what I have done.

Why Write?

One reason we hesitate to go where our writing takes us is uncertainty about why we write in the first place. At some point, all who do must reflect upon their reasons for writing. Every writer draws on a mixed bag of motives. Such motives not only drive writers but take courage to consider. Some are less than admirable. And it's usually the least admirable motives that keep working writers at their desk long after their more prudent colleagues have decided to teach school or sell insurance. "Writing a book is such a complicated, long-term, difficult process that all of the possible motives that can funnel in will," said William Gass, "and a great many of those motives will be base."

For public consumption, writers like to claim that they work in the service of art, creativity, and the public good. No writer who's given the matter serious consideration believes any such thing. H. L. Mencken thought the notion that authors were driven by aesthetic motives was absurd. Mencken called the writer one "in whom the normal vanity of all men is so vastly exaggerated that he finds it a sheer impossibility to hold it in. His overpowering impulse is to gyrate before his fellow men, flapping his wings and emitting defiant yells. This being forbidden by the police of all civilized countries, he takes it out by putting his yells on paper."

There is no basic difference between a writer's urge to put words on paper and that of DEENA to scrawl her name in wet sidewalk cement, or "The Duke" to spray-paint his nickname on city walls. A need for attention drives us. Recognition. Immortality. And why not? One of the most fundamental of human fears is that our existence will go unnoticed. We'd all like to have it recorded somewhere. What better way to achieve this goal than by writing? Long after maggots have had their way with my corpse, my name will still be on the spines of books in the Library of Congress. I'm *on the record*.

Writers mine energy sources wherever they find them; in their ego especially. The honest ones accept egotism as part of an author's job description. "It's a form of self-aggrandizement, writing at all, isn't it?" said Lawrence Durrell. When friends of E. B. White volunteered to read him whatever he liked after his eyesight failed, White chose to have them read his own collected works. "I have always been aware that I am by nature self-absorbed and egotistical," White admitted.

Self-absorption is an occupational hazard of writing. Or, should we say, a prerequisite. Why write at all if not to draw attention to one's self? Robert Frost thought a writer's prayer might be, "Oh, God, pay attention to me." At the Bread Loaf Writers' Conference one summer, Frost listened to Archibald MacLeish read poems to an enthusiastic audience. The warmer MacLeish's reception grew, the more restless Frost became. He began to play with some mimeographed notices that lay on a chair beside him. Now and again Frost arched a brow or waved a rolled-up paper impatiently at one of his rival's lines. Midway through the reading, Frost stage-whispered, "Archie's poems all have the same *tune*." The crackle of his paper grew louder. When MacLeish began reading an especially popular poem to his rapt listeners, a commotion erupted in Frost's vicinity. MacLeish stopped reading. Heads turned toward Frost. He was surrounded by billows of smoke. According to eyewitness Wallace Stegner, "playing around like an idle, inattentive schoolboy in a classroom, [Frost] had somehow contrived to strike a match and set fire to his handful of papers and was busy beating them out and waving away the smoke."

The narcissism of writers has often been noted (not least by writers themselves). What's seldom added is that it takes something as powerful as an unquenchable thirst for attention to trump the paralyzing fear of self-exposure. This doesn't mean that those who capitalize on egotism don't fear people paying attention to their inner life. They're just more afraid that no one will pay attention to them at all.

"There is nothing more dreadful to an author than neglect," said Samuel Johnson, "compared with which, reproach, hatred, and opposition are names of happiness; yet this worst, this meanest fate, everyone who dares to write has reason to fear." To avoid the risk of being ignored, writers will go to lengths others might regard as exhibitionism. James Jones thought that in their hunger for attention, writers were little different from "one of those guys who has a compulsion to take his thing out and show it on the street."

Were masks stripped away, we'd probably be startled by how many celebrated, accomplished individuals are driven by a need to show off. The intensity of this need can make the difference between working writers and those on leave. Far from being ashamed of their vanity, writers wrap it around themselves like Joseph's robe. In his classic essay "Why I Write," George Orwell put "sheer egotism" at the head of his list. "It is humbug to pretend that this is not a motive, and a strong one," wrote Orwell. "Writers share this characteristic with scientists, artists, politicians, lawyers, soldiers, successful businessmen—in short, with the whole top crust of humanity."

To Orwell, egotism meant "desire to seem clever, to be talked about, to be remembered after death, to get your own back on grown-ups who snubbed you in childhood, etc., etc." Like him, many write not just to show off but to show *them*. "Them" are the people in their past who said they couldn't do something. The art teacher who told Theodor Geisel (Dr. Seuss) that he'd never learn to draw. The twenty-three publishers who rejected Geisel's *And to Think That I Saw It on Mulberry Street*. The thirteen publishers who turned down William Kennedy's Pulitzer Prize–winning novel, *Ironweed*. The agent who refused to circulate Tony Hillerman's first Navajo-based mystery for fear it would ruin her reputation. Such doubters are potent goads. Kingsley Amis said that whenever he starts thinking about a new novel, part of his motive is "I'm going to show them this time. Without that, a lot of what passes under the name of creative energy would be lost."

Rejection early in life is gold to a writer. Garrison Keillor thought that those like him who were on the outs in high school are still trying to catch the eye of classmates who pretended they didn't exist. "You write for the people in high school who ignored you," agreed poet Carolyn Kizer. "We all do it." Writers don't necessarily want to smite those who smote them. I didn't write *Is There Life After High School?* to give my classmates grief. I wrote it in hopes that they'd take note, be impressed, and revise their opinion of me upward. Maybe they'd realize they should have asked me to sit at their table after all.

The anger implicit in a drive to show 'em is a rich source of energy. The fact that it's a negative source is neither here nor there. "I think that in order to write really well and convincingly, one must be somewhat poisoned by emotion," said Edna Ferber. "Dislike, displeasure, resentment, fault-finding, imagination, passionate remonstrance, a sense of injustice—they all make fine fuel."

A Pulitzer committee member once told me that they'd hesitated to award this prize to a gifted twenty-five-year-old because—based on past experience—they knew that winning a Pulitzer too young could make a subsequent career seem anticlimactic. Nobel laureates in literature seldom write anything major thereafter. Even though he was only forty-four when he won his Nobel, Albert Camus suffered severe writer's block afterward. Perhaps winning this prize is an antidote to bile. Writers with a Nobel on their shelf have been deprived of their anger. They no longer have anything to prove; no " 'em" to show. Many authors simply can't write when they feel that highly esteemed. William Gass, for one, maintained that he worked best when he was "on the page, very combative, very hostile. . . . I write because I hate. A lot. Hard. . . . I wish to make my hatred acceptable because my hatred is much of me, if not the best part."

Like many writers, Gass found that a hunger for revenge—*getting even*—consumed him. To make this point, the novelist cited a line he'd put in the mouth of a character: "I want to rise so high that when I shit I won't miss anybody." A passion to *get even* is the surly cousin of a need to show 'em. Vengefulness wants not just to impress but to vanquish old foes. It's quite common among writers. In an essay on James Joyce, biographer Leon Edel argued that *Ulysses*'s author wrote "not for literature but for personal revenge." Is this motive base? Probably. So what? For one thing, it's being exercised only on paper. No one is killed, maimed, or imprisoned by a writer's vengeful words. For another, wanting to get even with tormentors from one's past is a first-rate motivator. "The good thing about writing fiction," said lawyer-novelist John Grisham, "is that you can get back at people. I've gotten back at lawyers, prosecutors, judges, law professors, and politicians. I just line 'em up and shoot 'em."

Grisham is not the only one. In the midst of a bitter divorce, Sue Grafton incorporated fantasies of getting back at her ex-husband into the text of a mystery. Stephen King took revenge on the man who'd revealed a pseudonym he was using by bumping him off in his next novel. Elmore Leonard had his way with Hollywood types who'd mutilated his books on the screen by creating clownlike moviemakers in *Stick* and *Get Shorty*.

High school classmates—those who torment the type of student who later becomes a writer—are a common target for revenge. Think of all the literature savaging high school's elite: *Rabbit Run*, *The Catcher in the Rye*, *The Last Picture Show*. Is this intentional? Of course it is. Larry McMurtry—who, according to his high school's principal, "was not accepted by the majority of his classmates"—later inscribed a classmate's copy of *The Last Picture Show*, "Revenge is sweet."

Lonely Kids, Lovely Writers

Successful writers rarely emerge from the ranks of the popular. Those who went to the prom seldom take up the pen. Why should they? Their thirst for attention has been slaked. They don't have as many scores to settle. Most of all, writing poses too great a threat to the feeling of popularity that's been branded on their psyche.

Larry L. King once wrote of a classmate who'd won the Most Likely to Succeed award King thought should have been his, "I coveted his deep voice, easy laugh, smooth social patter, constant cheer. Kent made people smile. I seemed to make them nervous." Writers routinely make this type of observation about their young selves. "I was despised and hated by the boys," said Samuel Taylor Coleridge. George Orwell recalled being a lonely child with "disagreeable mannerisms which made me unpopular throughout my schooldays."

In her novel *Lives of Girls and Women*, Alice Munro portrays a bookish high school girl named Del who lives in the town of Jubilee. As Del walks with her science-whiz friend Jerry along a trestle,

> a car full of people from the class passed underneath, hooting at us, and I did have a vision, as if from outside, of how strange this was—Jerry contemplating and welcoming a future that would annihilate Jubilee and life in it, and I myself planning secretly to turn it into black fable and tie it up in my novel, and the town, the people who really were the town, just hooting car horns—to mock anybody walking, not riding, on a Sunday afternoon—and never knowing what danger they were in from us.

Those words could not have been written by a popular teenager. Not only would she lack the anger to write them, but she'd have something precious to lose: her ingrained sense of status. The worst thing that can befall aspiring writers is winning the popularity that might be endangered by words they put on paper. Popular people don't wish to give offense. What human being would? Movie director George Cukor once said that likability was an actor's ruination. The sensation of being *liked*, he explained, was so addictive that it led to winning portrayals devoid of depth, candor, or daring. Popularity is a serious brake on artistic expression of any kind. If people like you—and you expect them to like you—the risk of doing anything controversial, or saying anything revealing, is profound.

Feeling unpopular as a child gets one in shape for serious

writing. This is true for a number of reasons. Misfits spend a lot of time alone. Future writers use that time to make up imaginary playmates. As outsiders, they develop a habit of observing others. And being rejected by other kids not only fills young authors-to-be with grievances in need of redress but gets them used to being disliked. That puts them in a very strong artistic position. Putting people off feels like business as usual.

Like many, I've often been disappointed when meeting a writer whose work I admire, only to find that person off-putting. Some are downright obnoxious. How could such an unpleasant human being write with such sensitivity, such insight, and candor? Or are the two connected? Perhaps rudeness and the courage to put your work on public display are symbiotic. An ability to reveal unattractive parts of yourself on the page and in person dips from the same well. That's why it's not necessarily a bad thing for a writer to lack social grace. "You may rely on it you have the best of me in my books," wrote Henry David Thoreau to a reader who wanted to meet him, "and that I am not worth seeing personally, the stuttering, blundering, clod-hopper that I am."

On the eve of *Main Street*'s publication, H. L. Mencken and George Jean Nathan met Sinclair Lewis at a party. After Lewis told them (among other things) that he was "the best writer in this here gottdamn country," Mencken and Nathan fled the party. "Of all the idiots I've ever laid eyes on," said Mencken after they took refuge in a tavern, "that fellow is the worst!" Three days later, Mencken wrote Nathan: "Grab hold of the bar-rail, steady yourself, and prepare yourself for a terrible shock! I've just read the advance sheets of the book of that Lump we met . . . and, by God, he has done the job! It's a genuinely excellent piece of work. Get it as soon as you can and take a look. I begin to believe that perhaps there isn't a God after all."

Something I've often discussed with colleagues is how one's social skills atrophy after spending so much time alone. Frederick Exley thought that those who write eventually reach a point outside human relationships; that they become, in a sense, "ahuman." He probably spoke for himself. Exley was revered by many of his colleagues, not so much because he was a good writer (though he was) but because he was a bold writer. Only a colleague could appreciate how many risks Exley took in his fictional memoirs. "Writers of every kind of aesthetic and cultural persuasion discuss its moments with one another as sports fans compare favorite plays," said novelist Geoffrey Wolff of *A Fan's Notes*. The writing in this book was uneven, but its candor wasn't. Exley's novel-memoir was a flawed, offensive, and dead honest report of his life in and out of the asylum. Its author seemed to hold nothing back: his failures as a son and father, his drunkenness, his time spent alone on a couch brooding about the New York Giants and their running back Frank Gifford.

In one passage, Exley wrote about leaving his couch to interview for jobs. Although these memories were fifteen years old, he wrote, "even now, at the oddest moments, taking a shower or petting a stray dog, I will suddenly remember, hardly knowing whether to thunder with laughter or hide my head under a pillow."

> If I was kept waiting beyond a carefully scrutinized five minutes, there was no interview! Rising from my chair and ambling over to the man's

secretary, I would bow ever so slightly, the very
image of genteel breeding; then suddenly, bring-
ing myself up to a dictatorially rigid posture, I
would proclaim, my tone controlled but testy:
"I'm sorry, young lady, but will you tell your
employer that Mr. Exley had other commitments
and couldn't wait. If he wishes to set up another
appointment and begin it at the—ah—
designated time"—I would be looking at my
empty wrist as though it contained a hundred-
jewel job—"then he knows where to reach me."
Clicking my heels slightly and smiling my distant
smile, I would depart, saying, *"Adieu,* my dear,
adieu," terribly certain I had rendered the girl
sexually tractable.

Although he lacked the elegance of an Updike or range
of a Mailer, Exley was painfully honest in a way readers
couldn't miss. He made an art form of his boorishness, on
and off the page. Exley was in bad odor among editors and
reviewers because he called them drunkenly at odd hours to
plead that they take mercy on him and his work. Many
considered this a gross violation of publishing etiquette. But
anyone who's written for publication has wanted to do the
same thing. And what if Exley did routinely cross lines of
propriety? He may have been crude and inappropriate, but
this had no bearing on his ability as a writer. Quite the
contrary. The same qualities that at times sent Frederick
Exley whimpering to the psych ward also drove him to the
typewriter with a seeming inability to tell us anything less
than his whole story.

The writer as obnoxious goofball is a stereotype cultivated not least by writers themselves. (Writers' spouses might be excused for thinking it's a license to abuse alcohol and ignore their families.) According to this stereotype, when not off on benders or attempting suicide, writers are prone to muttering darkly about sundry grievances and offending people they love. Kurt Vonnegut went so far as to say writers make a living from their mental disease. "It's a nervous work," agreed novelist Shirley Hazzard. "The state that you need to write is the state that others are paying large sums to get rid of."

The act of recording one's thoughts for publication is so unsettling that to summon the necessary courage it helps to lack social grace. Rude writers can be more open because they see no alternative. They're beyond caring what anyone thinks about them. Indifference to the opinion of others makes it easier to report directly whatever one sees, hears, touches, smells, and feels. Boorishness can help writers transcend inhibition and say what's on their mind. It's one of many less-than-pristine traits that helps them find the courage to write.

All of these factors—rudeness, mixed motives, and a need to look inside and report what one sees—are part and parcel of that courage. This reality has a lot to do with why writers can behave in such peculiar ways. And why they talk as much about the bravery writing takes as the talent. Like anyone else, writers don't always feel very brave. And—being imaginative people—they often find creative ways to cope with their fears.

II

Coming to Terms with Fear

· · · · · · · · · ·

5

Finessing Fear

> Speech was given to man
> to disguise his thoughts.
> — *Voltaire*

*L*awrence Block spent a long apprenticeship producing hack fiction. Too long. After he wrote a mainstream novel in the early 1960s, a Random House editor suggested some changes. This made Block angry. He withdrew the manuscript and went back to writing potboilers. It took Block years to realize that the real reason he hadn't responded to this editor's suggestions was fear that he couldn't pull the project off. As he finally concluded, his anger at her "was simply a smokescreen I had thrown up to conceal my fear from myself." It would be another fourteen years before Lawrence Block started writing the Matt Scudder mysteries that won him critical acclaim and devoted readers. "Fear is the mind-killer," he concluded, "and unacknowledged fear is the worst kind."

Fear is a great poseur. Men especially are loath to admit that they're scared, even to themselves. Instead they convert anxiety into more acceptable feelings (anger, usually).

Writers of both sexes are seldom conscious of the many occasions when fear guides their hand. They deny it even to themselves. But this doesn't alleviate anxiety. It merely fobs it off onto the unconscious. One result is writer's block: the unconscious mind exercising its right to remain silent even as the conscious one wonders what in the heck is going on.

A writing block is little more than the brain's sensible section flashing: DANGER AHEAD. STOP! "Writer's block is a misnomer," said Tom Wolfe. "What's called writer's block is almost always ordinary fear." The connection between fear and writer's block has often been noted. What's less obvious is how commonly work produced by active writers can be distorted by anxiety. The inner censors who feed on fear can be every bit as onerous as a Soviet commissar. They subject us to a form of literary parole in which we're allowed to write but only on condition that we avoid topics we care about deeply, and never say anything too clearly.

Authors routinely, if unknowingly, calm their nerves by producing less than their best. This is most often accomplished by building sturdy walls of obscure words and complex sentences to protect themselves from critical eyes. Other tactics include writing for their own eyes only, or those of a select few, or by being content to plan on "doing some writing" at some future date that never seems to arrive.

Nonwriting, Trunk Writing, and Privishing

Not writing at all constitutes the ultimate triumph of fear. We seldom admit this, however, even to ourselves. We just can't seem to "get around to it." That sounds like writer's block and sometimes is. Unlike blocked writers, however—who try to put words on paper but can't—

nonwriting writers have stopped trying. "Maybe after I retire I'll get back to it," they may say. Or: "when the kids are grown"; "when I have a better office to write in"; "once I've bought a new computer"; "after I take another writing class."

Fear is a tough adversary. It takes more than mere skills or better tools to keep anxiety from running—or ruining—our show. Imagining that extra preparation makes for better writing is like assuming that the more books we read on weight loss, the thinner we'll become. It's understandable to think, "If only I had a good agent, I wouldn't be so scared." Or, "I won't really be able to write until I get a proper fellowship." Or, "Damn this clunky old computer, anyway. No wonder I can't get any writing done." Understandable and self-deluding. Rather than paddle boldly into the rapids of our fears we search desperately for ways to portage around them. This leads to a search for what I call *false fear busters*: tactics that soothe writing nerves in the short run but do nothing in the long run to help us actually write. False fear busters include:

- buying new gear (computer, typewriter, fountain pen)
- moving to a more pleasant setting (locale, office, etc.)
- attending writers' conferences *in lieu of writing*
- imagining that a good agent will solve our problems
- applying for grants and fellowships
- developing an elaborate, evasive prose style
- improving our vocabulary
- engaging in plausible procrastination (extra research, detailed outlines, one more draft)
- finding excuses for not writing (dog needs walking, plants need watering, house needs cleaning, etc.)

I've sometimes been tempted to distribute sheets of paper in writing workshops that read "I'd have been a great writer except _____." Everyone has compelling reasons for not producing the writing they've dreamed of doing. An aspiring author once told me a heartrending story of having all his manuscripts stolen from a U-Haul parked outside a Phoenix motel as he moved from California to New York. This destroyed his writing morale. As a result, he'd spent the last few years selling cars and was just now struggling to regain his will to write.

The parable of the lost manuscript is surprisingly common. I've been told by any number of discouraged writers that they lost their will along with a manuscript. All writers are grateful for a good excuse not to write. Losing work is among the best. But those who are determined to write won't let even the catastrophe of a lost manuscript deter them.

• Nearly every copy of Ernest Hemingway's early fiction was in a suitcase stolen from the train his wife, Hadley, was taking from Paris to Lausanne. Hemingway searched frantically for carbons. None could be found. He subsequently developed a morbid, if understandable fear of losing manuscripts. But this fear didn't stop him from writing new ones. At times Hemingway even thought he was a better writer for having been unburdened of his amateurish early efforts.

• When T. E. Lawrence left his first draft of *Seven Pillars of Wisdom* in a train station, he exulted, "I've lost the damned thing!" Although Lawrence had already destroyed the notes on which it was based, he eventually was persuaded to rewrite the now classic book.

· Thomas Carlyle loaned John Stuart Mill his only copy of the first volume of *The French Revolution*. A servant of Mill's mistook Carlyle's manuscript for wastepaper and threw it in the fire. When Mill—"pale as Hector's ghost"—told his friend of the calamity, Carlyle was nonplussed. "I felt in general that I was as a little schoolboy," he wrote his brother, "who had laboriously written out his *Copy* as he could, and was showing it not without satisfaction to the Master: but lo! the Master had suddenly torn it, saying: 'No, boy, thou must go and write it *better*.' What could I do but sorrowing go and try to obey?"

Losing work is almost a rite of passage among authors. Gail Godwin sent her only copy of an early novel to a London publisher whose address proved to be an empty building. The only computer disk containing a book draft by Maxine Hong Kingston was consumed in the Oakland fires of 1991. An early draft of Steinbeck's *Of Mice and Men* was partly chewed to pieces by his dog, Toby.

Jeffrey Konitz dedicated his novel *The Guardian* "To Rufus, who edited Chapter 27." According to Konitz, his Great Pyrenees ate that chapter, forcing him to write a better one. That's the attitude of a working writer. He's as desperate as anyone for reasons not to write, but only up to a point. It's natural to find excuses—real or contrived—to avoid writing. Scribbling words on paper hour after hour, month after month, year after year with only anxiety for company is an unnatural act. Finding reasons not to engage in this act could be seen as a sign of mental health. That's why writers need to be vigilant against such excuses, if they'd rather be actual than hypothetical writers.

One way to avoid writing without giving up the dream altogether is to talk about the words one *intends* to write . . . eventually . . . when conditions are right. This approach is nearly guaranteed to keep one from actually doing so. Fiction writers find that telling stories usually dissipates the energy needed to write them. Anne Tyler said that when garrulous would-be writers start telling her their tales, "I want to almost physically reach over and cover their mouths and say, 'You'll lose it if you're not careful.' " Amy Tan learned this lesson the hard way. Tan had to set aside two half-completed manuscripts after she'd discussed the books so exhaustively that she lost the will to write them.

Another popular way to relieve writing anxiety is to put words on paper, but not for public consumption. I know this from rummaging through the many cartons and trunks of my ancestors' possessions in our basement. Inside them are a remarkable number of manuscripts—stories, essays, plays, poems—but hardly any letters of acceptance or rejection from publishers. My ancestors were trunk writers. They wrote for their own eyes only. Trunk writing has a certain intellectual integrity. Not one comma has to be changed to please an editor or court a reader. But it's seldom an alternative chosen with enthusiasm. Any writer wants her work to be *read*, by lots of readers. Trunk writers would like to be published too, if only this didn't mean risking rejection and feeling so *exposed*. Many, perhaps most, writers—including some of the most gifted—never dare to find out what will happen if they let their literary children leave home to make their way in the world.

Some trunk writers show their work to selected readers. Many an unmailed story or poem is pressed on friends and relatives. Their typical response is, "I like this." By that, they usually mean, "I love you and wouldn't hurt you for the world." Writers who circulate their work among a few unthreatening readers are publishing; they're just not doing a good job of it. This is more like *privishing*. It resembles the samizdat of Soviet writers whose only means of getting their work out was to circulate it in typescript. But unlike writers who are oppressed by the state, free citizens who privish are oppressed only by their own anxiety.

Writing at all takes courage. Submitting work for publication takes something closer to bravado. Actually putting words on paper and mailing them could lead to the discovery that one's writing won't get published. Then the dream is in peril. But is it better not to learn this? To keep a fantasy alive by never putting it to the test? Many do. They're among our best writers. They don't lack talent. Nor are they self-deprecating. Some have the highest estimate of their own work. All they need is the courage to step forward and ask if others agree.

There is an alternative. That alternative is writing for publication, but on such obscure terms that readers will feel too ignorant to criticize.

Literary Fog

A Dr. Myron L. Fox once spoke to a group of psychiatrists, psychologists, and educators on "Mathematical Game Theory as Applied to Physician Education." A tape of Dr. Fox's hour-long lecture was later shown to two other groups of professionals. On follow-up questionnaires, most who heard his talk judged it clear and stimulating. In fact, "Dr. Fox" was an actor hired by three researchers to speak in double-talk. Their goal was to discover if well-educated listeners would admit that they couldn't understand an incomprehensible lecture. None did. "Considering the educational sophistication of the subjects," the researchers observed, "it is striking that none of them detected the lecture for what it was."

Such an episode suggests why the most popular fear buster of all is to write, but not well. Instead of their best, writers who take this approach give us jargon, adjectives, adverbs, passive verbs, qualifying words, and run-on sentences. Why do so many do this? Don't they know better? Of course they do. But producing verbal confusion provides relief from anxiety.

> Like fear of prophecies contained in dreams,
> the fear of writing down eternal words
> is the real reason for verbosity.
> — *Yevgeny Yevtushenko*

Inflated language, obscure references, and needlessly complex sentences surround their authors with a dense cloud of verbal fog. Sometimes the fog is so thick that one can't see through it to the writer. That's the whole idea. Those who generate fog are Wizards of Oz hoping desperately that nobody pulls the curtain to reveal a trembling little writer behind it. This seldom happens. Readers who dare to point out that incomprehensible writing can't be comprehended risk being told that the problem is theirs. Opacity also permits authors to be moving targets. If their message can't be deciphered, how can it be criticized?

Readers don't necessarily think less of writers who produce fog. Nor do critics necessarily, or colleagues. At worst they'll assume that the problem is theirs; that they're too thick to grasp such profundity. When the English writer Douglas Jerrold was sent an advance copy of Robert Browning's poem *Sordello*, he read the poem eagerly, only to realize that it made no sense to him. "Oh, God, I *am* an idiot," Jerrold told himself. He showed Browning's poem to his wife. After reading it through, she said, "I don't understand what this man means. It is gibberish." Though few readers dared to express themselves with her candor, Mrs. Jerrold wasn't the only one who had this reaction. When members of the London Poetry Society asked Browning to interpret a particularly difficult passage of *Sordello*, he read it twice, frowned, then admitted, "When I wrote that, God and I knew what I meant, but now God alone knows."

Rather than risk sounding dense, readers, colleagues, and critics who can't figure out what a writer is trying to say but think it sounds intelligent will typically resort to calling such work "daring," "provocative," or "complex." An unholy alliance of writers and readers is at work here. Should anyone dare to raise questions about her hard-to-grasp writing, the author can brush these responses aside by saying "that person missed the point" (i.e., unlike me and a few friends of mine, he hasn't got a clue). This shifts the focus from the author's writing to the reader's intellect. Having the option to respond that way helps explain why obscurity is such a popular writing style. Either the writer will be called profound by those who can't decipher her work but don't dare to admit this; or, should a brave soul call her art artless, that critic can himself be called thick. The writer collects at either end.

The formidable Gertrude Stein spent years passing off wordplay as literature on this basis. Although few readers could decipher Stein's literary cryptography, she was lionized nonetheless. Her "experimental" writing was lauded for its inventiveness. This included Stein-lines such as, "If the red is rose and there is a gate surrounding it, if inside is let in and there places change then certainly something is upright." And, "A virgin a whole virgin is judged made and so between curves and outlines and real seasons and more out glasses and a perfectly unprecedented arrangement between old ladies and mild colds there is no satin wood shining."

Gertrude Stein's publisher, Bennett Cerf, once interviewed her on national radio. Cerf suggested that this would be a good opportunity for Stein to tell the American public what her writing was all about. "I'm very proud to be your publisher," he said, "but as I've always told you, I don't understand much of what you're saying." Replied Stein, "Well, I've always told you, Bennett, you're a very nice boy but you're rather stupid."

As Cerf discovered, anyone who calls fog fog risks being told it's he who has a problem. That's a colossal risk to take. It's one reason that garbled writing is such a balm to writer's nerves. Should some brave reader of confused syntax say, "I don't get this," the writer is free to respond (or at least think), "You wouldn't." By contrast, a clear, direct, vigorous piece of writing invites a clear, direct, vigorous response. That could be, "This stinks." Or, "Whoever wrote this piece of garbage is not someone I'd care to know." The fear of inviting such a response helps explain why so little writing gets produced that is clear, direct, and vigorous. Fuzzy writing may not be fun to read, but it's harder to pin down. I've heard other writers talk about the fear of being *mis*apprehended. I'm far more scared of being *apprehended*; of having people understand what I'm trying to say, but just not care for my message.

The boldest writers of all are those who leave no doubt in the reader's mind about what they're getting at. These writers have no wiggle room: no path to escape, to reinterpret, or to claim their ideas were too complex for simple minds. Clarity raises the stakes of an already daring activity. "It is always a thrilling risk to say exactly what you mean," said Patricia Hampl, "to express exactly what you see."

In his book *Doublespeak*, William Lutz cites a model of clear, daring prose from an annual report issued by Teradyne, Inc. This report told stockholders that Teradyne's sales were down 9 percent, "which doesn't sound so bad when you say it fast, except that it followed a 14 percent drop . . . , for our first two-year decline ever. The fact that most of our competition did even worse is some consolation. But not much, frankly."

Or consider Jill Robinson's self-portrait in her memoir, *Bed/Time/Story*:

> I put on several different outfits. The advantage
> of not knowing who you are is you can attempt
> to be all things to all men . . . or women. My
> mother saw me always glancing in every mirror,
> every window; in the gleaming blades of knives.
> She said, "Jill is vain." She did not know I was
> looking to see who would be there this time.

One would think we'd prefer clear, direct statements such as these to garbled ones that "sound" deep. This isn't always true. Plainness and simplicity are admired more in

Shaker furniture than in written words. Clear, simple writing risks being called simpleminded by those who are unsure of their own intellectual gifts. It's a variation on Groucho Marx's line about not wanting to join any club that would have him: anything I can grasp easily couldn't possibly be profound. That's one reason the market for obscure writing is so robust. Readability is no prerequisite for either commercial or literary success. An editor at a major publisher once confided to Joyce Carol Oates that she couldn't even finish a noted writer's latest novel. Oates couldn't either. That book went on to win several awards. To test the hypothesis that opacity didn't hinder sales, a researcher inserted printed slips of paper three-quarters of the way through seventy copies of two popular but turgid books at a bookstore. These pieces of paper offered five dollars to anyone who called the researcher's phone number and said she'd reached that point in the book. Nobody called.

There's little penalty for obscure writing, and much potential reward. This, more than ignorance of technique, is the real reason so much "bafflegab" gets set in type. It's seldom a result of stupidity or even ignorance on the part of the writer. Anyone bright enough to write at all usually knows how to communicate. Few have trouble doing so in person. They simply prefer not to be clear on paper, and for very good reasons. "The very vagueness of abstract words is one of the reasons for their popularity," suggests Sir Ernest Gowers in his book *Plain Words*. "To express one's thoughts accurately is hard work, and to be precise is sometimes dangerous."

Higher Obfuscation

At West Point, Dwight Eisenhower's instructors praised his papers for their clarity. Later, Eisenhower wrote lucid, well-crafted histories of European campaigns for the Battle Monuments Commission. As president, however, Ike made an art form of garbled syntax. This was no accident. "Don't worry," he said when press secretary James Hagerty expressed concern about a ticklish question that might be asked at a press conference. "If it comes up, I'll confuse them."

We're all born with an ability to get our message across. The ability to baffle is acquired. Although I often hear about programs in "effective communication" and the like, I've seldom met anyone who couldn't make a point he really wanted to make. "Communication problems" usually result from a prayer that others won't get our message so that we can keep our options open. ("That isn't what I meant.") Saying exactly what we mean can be risky. That's why we so seldom do.

Safe	*Risky*
You may feel some discomfort.	This is going to hurt.
I'm experiencing some anger.	I'm mad.
He's having trouble communicating.	I can't make heads or tails out of what he's saying.
She altered her verbal response pattern.	She lied.

The last example comes from terminology used by sexologists William Masters and Virginia Johnson. Perhaps because they explored such dangerous territory, Masters and Johnson were expert obfuscators. In *Human Sexual Inadequacy* they write about a couple whose marriage foundered because of infidelity: "In retrospect, had sufficient information been exchanged to relieve their intense anxieties and to enlist a return of interpersonal communication, there is every reason to believe that in view of their mutual level of sexual responsivity outside of marriage and the definitive residual of interpersonal concern present at the time of therapy, the innate levels of their mutual responsivity could have been concentrated in the marital bed." Historian Paul Robinson translated that long, incomprehensible sentence into a short, clear one: "Since they were successful with other partners yet still cared for each other, a frank confession would probably have resolved their problem." Robinson also translated the following terms used by Masters and Johnson:

interdigitate	combine
vocalize	say
potentiator	cause
the sexual unit	couple

Since they were writing about such a volatile topic, Masters and Johnson might be forgiven for cloaking their findings in obscure language. This lent them a greater measure of safety than had they expressed themselves in livelier, more accessible terms.

Writing teachers usually emphasize the need for clear, active forms of expression. Such forms give vigor to writing. They're also dangerous, on or off the page. In families, communities, and organizations, forthright talk can lead to conflict. With their emphasis on consensus, societies such as the Japanese encourage indirect forms of communication. So do small towns everywhere and most bureaucracies. Direct, active statements are the style of a loner (e.g., a writer). Precise words convey unmistakably what an individual believes, regardless of social dogma. In group settings, this can be hazardous. As a college professor once admitted to a restive audience, "I'm afraid I've made myself too clear."

Harry Truman was often in hot water because he left so little doubt in listeners' minds about what he was getting at. Truman—who never attended college—expressed himself in vivid, down-to-earth terms. "Being a president is like riding a tiger," he once said. "A man has to keep on riding or be swallowed." Truman's speak-your-mind quality made him a good, lucid writer. On November 1, 1949, he made the following entry in his diary:

> Had dinner by myself tonight. Worked in the Lee House office until dinner time. A butler came in very formally and said, "Mr. President, dinner is served." I walk into the dining room in the Blair House. Barnett in tails and white tie pulls out my chair, pushes me up to the table. John in tails and white tie brings me a fruit cup. Barnett takes away the empty cup. John brings me a plate, Barnett brings me a tenderloin, John brings me asparagus, Barnett brings me carrots and beets. I have to eat alone and in silence in candle-lit room. I ring. Barnett takes the plate and butter plates. John comes in with a napkin

and silver crumb tray—there are no crumbs but John has to brush them off the table anyway. Barnett brings me a plate with a finger bowl and doily on it. I remove the finger bowl and doily and John puts a glass saucer and a little bowl on the plate. Barnett brings me some chocolate custard. John brings me a demitasse (at home a little cup of coffee—about two good gulps) and my dinner is over. I take a hand bath in the finger bowl and go back to work.

What a life!

It's generally assumed that we'd rather write and read clear prose such as this. If that's so, where did all the bafflegab come from? The most common explanation is that those who produce it haven't learned their lessons. Maybe they need to take a course on how to write better. That's the wrong solution to the right problem. Bad writers can usually do better; they simply prefer not to. Most function in settings where plain talk not only isn't *en*couraged but is actively *dis*couraged. Far from fostering clarity, the average bureaucracy, corporation, or educational institution rewards obscurity. It does this in ways that make sense only to members of that organization. Language serves many masters in group settings. Communication is only one goal, and not always the most important one. Even more important is to indicate by repeated use of insider terms that one is a member of the tribe. Neotribal prose is filled with words and phrases that make sense only to insiders. Outsiders don't get it. That's the whole idea. Regular use of insider words confirms and reconfirms that one belongs to a group whose members *do* get it.

Consider the sentence "A multi-purpose thrust in a problematic area does not appear to be conducive to time efficiency." That thought came from a committee of educators. Presumably it made sense to them, but it doesn't to the rest of us. Nor does the following line from a university publication: "The functional methodology shall be based on an inter-disciplinary process model, which employs a lateral feed-back syndrome across a sanction-constituency interface, coupled with a circular-spiral recapitulatory function for variable-flux accommodation and policy modification."

Neotribal writing is just as common in educational institutions as in any other, if not more so. Colleges and universities are citadels of writing-as-ritual. I always warn college students that following my recommendation to write clearly and simply may hurt their grades in other classes. As a test of this hypothesis, I once gave another faculty member—a psychologist—some papers written for me by college freshmen. Invariably the psychologist disparaged those I thought were clear and praised pieces of writing that struck me as confused. In a systematic study of the same phenomenon, two professors in Chicago had high school and college English teachers rate essays that were identical in content but not in style. In almost every instance these teachers preferred the ones that were deliberately written to be wordy and vague over those that were lucid and direct.

While studying for his Ph.D. at the University of Virginia, Richard Bullock—now director of writing programs at Ohio's Wright State University—taught undergraduates how to express themselves more clearly. A sociology major came to him with the opposite problem. This student had found that clear writing was hurting her grades. One professor in particular was flunking her papers. He wanted them to incorporate more "scholarly language (i.e., jargon)." She needed to pass his course to graduate. Bullock was faced with a dilemma. He knew what kind of prose his colleague wanted. It just violated everything he believed about good, direct writing. But encouraging his tutee to keep writing clearly meant she might not graduate. So Bullock taught her how to write with lots of jargon, abstractions, and passive-tense verbs. She passed the course and graduated.

Toward the end of my own senior year in college, I reread my freshman papers. I thought this would be amusing since I'd learned so much about writing in the interim. To my horror, these early efforts were clearly superior to the later ones. They were lively, concrete, engaging. After years of training and modeling by professors, I'd mastered the arts of passivity, vagueness, and abstraction. It took two years as a newspaper reporter to regain a more active voice. Later, I worked as a magazine editor. My job was to rewrite pro-fessors' manuscripts in plain English. This usually caused great anguish to the original authors. The problem wasn't their pride of authorship so much as an accurate apprehen-sion of the danger I'd put them in. Stripped of code words and convoluted sentences in their original manuscripts, they stood to lose considerable prestige among academic colleagues.

According to Professor J. Scott Armstrong of the Uni-versity of Pennsylvania, among academics, "obtuse writing . . . seems to yield higher prestige for the author." Arm-strong has conducted a number of studies to test this hy-pothesis. In one, he asked twenty management professors to identify the more prestigious of two unidentified journals presented to them. The more readable journal (as deter-mined by the Flesch Reading Ease Test) was judged the least prestigious. In another experiment, Armstrong rewrote the same journal article in two different forms. One he rated confusing and convoluted, the other concise and clear. A panel of thirty-two professors agreed that the confusing version reported a higher level of research. "Overall, the evidence is consistent with a common suspicion," concluded Armstrong. "Clear communication of one's research is not appreciated. Faculty are impressed by less readable articles."

In a speech to the Association of American University Presses, Patricia Nelson Limerick, a history professor at the University of Colorado, tried to make sense of her colleagues' preference for intellectual jive talk. Limerick thought it was a product of their timidity. "Professors are often shy, timid and even fearful people," she told her audience, "and under those circumstances, dull, difficult prose can function as a kind of protective camouflage." From graduate school on, Limerick explained, career academics learn that terrible sanctions can be imposed on those who express themselves in ways that make sense beyond the academy's walls. Academics therefore protect themselves by defending cautious ideas with insider words, complicated syntax, and qualifying phrases such as "a case might be made" and "one could argue that."

To timidity, one might add laziness as a reason for generating fog. Saying exactly what one means is hard work. Being vague is far easier. Endless revisions are sometimes necessary to clarify an idea. (Ernest Hemingway thought the real reason Gertrude Stein's writing made so little sense was that she wouldn't do the tedious rewriting necessary to make it intelligible.) Like most writers, I find my early drafts are filled with generalities and clichés. This is usually because I hadn't yet taken the time to hone my point. Bafflegab is like Pascal's long letter; he hadn't time to write a short one. When my writing is vague, passive, and confusing, it's nearly always a sign that I'm tired, lazy, or scared (sometimes all three). I had neither the energy nor the heart to penetrate my own fog. The rough-draft quality of impenetrable writing can soothe authors' nerves. If you haven't given writing your best shot, and the results are criticized, you're free to say, "Shoot, I could have done better if I'd taken the time. That's just something I dashed off." If you do write your best, and your best gets panned, there is no place to run to or hide. Far more bad writing than we appreciate can be traced back to a lethal combination of laziness and cowardice on the part of the writer.

A writer who isn't clear has work to do. If a reader doesn't "get" what he's saying, it's the *writer's* problem, not the reader's. This is seldom considered true in academic institutions or literary circles, which prize their eliteness. Perhaps this is why so many clear, vigorous writers didn't have literary backgrounds: Churchill, Darwin, Freud, Einstein; Stephen Jay Gould and Lewis Thomas in our own time. "I never study style," said Darwin of his approach to writing; "all that I do is try to get the subject as clear as I can in my head, and express it in the commonest language that occurs to me. But I generally have to think a good deal before the simplest arrangement occurs to me."

To remind students that no one has a monopoly on good writing, I sometimes read aloud from the back of a little bottle of insect repellent:

> **Don't goop on.** Three drops for hands and face
> is plenty. Rub in well. For chiggers apply spar-

ingly on tops of shoes and socks and along open-
ings of clothing. Repeat as needed. Special
Cream Formula goes into pores: lasts longer;
won't be sticky, stinky, or greasy; won't injure
guns, tackle, or clothes when used as directed.

My students and I analyze this piece of writing. The
smallness of its forum enforces economy of expression.
That's good. Also, the "Directions" genre calls for (but
seldom gets) such clear, active language. We pause to worry
over *goop*. Is this word too colloquial? Does it call too much
attention to itself? No better alternative suggests itself. *Goop*
gives a graphic picture of the act in question. So *goop* it is.
Stinky is another venturesome term that does its job, and
stands in poetic juxtaposition to the word *sticky*. This piece
of writing is a success. It's clear. It's vigorous. It has good
rhythm. The writer accomplished her mission.

Unlike what nonwriters often believe, good writing
does not require a big vocabulary. E. B. White thought one
of his blessings as a writer was the fact that his limited
vocabulary didn't permit him to use obscure words. Mark
Twain had a similar perspective. "I never write *metropolis* for
seven cents because I can get the same price for *city*," said
Twain. "I never write *policeman* because I can get the same
money for *cop*." Insecure writers want to show off their
vocabulary from fear of sounding ignorant. If I don't use
obscure words, they seem to wonder, how will readers
know that I have a college degree? If I do use simple words,
won't people think I'm a simpleton? Such attitudes make
for deadly writing. Readers sent too often to the dictionary
soon set aside the book that drove them there and pick up
another one (or, worse yet, turn on the television). Ornate

language is usually a tipoff that an author wasn't sure what he wanted to say, or didn't dare. Confident writers have the courage to speak plainly; to let their thoughts shine rather than their vocabulary. "Short words are best," advised Churchill, "and the old words when short are best of all."

Transcending Craft

Here is the dilemma, then: to write well, we must express ourselves clearly and risk rejection. We can finesse this risk by generating fog. Doing so, however, means we'll never achieve our potential as writers. To the degree that we can confront and transcend a fear of exposing ourselves on the page—any page—our writing will improve. That's one reason such gripping writing grows out of crisis; occasions when we no longer care how we're coming across and just *write*. When we write about topics that touch us deeply— illness, loss, death—our language usually becomes spare and direct.

After his father died, Los Angeles screenwriter Burt Prelutsky wrote:

> This afternoon, we buried my father. I didn't think I would, but I shed tears. I cried because he had worked too hard for too long for too little. For many years I had resented him because he had never told me he loved me; now I wept because I'd never told him.

When she was sixteen, author Faye Moskowitz sat beside her mother's body, flooded by memories:

I remembered the bas-relief of shame, the evening I came home from somewhere to find her leaning on the kitchen sink, washing a stack of dishes I had left undone. "Shut up!" I had shouted when she spoke to me, angered at the robe and slippers, the cane lying on the floor, the medicine bottle, accouterments of a mother too sick to care for her own. Now we were cut off in midsentence. Now I would never be able to tell her how sorry I was for everything.

No one has trouble being lucid when they are sufficiently moved. Those who are willing to say what they want and take the consequences seldom have difficulty being clear, compelling, and to the point. Confronting writing anxiety this way gives us the means to grasp and transcend the real problem with which we're dealing rather than resort to craft. Skill alone makes it too easy to write *around* what we have to say; to build a fortress of words that is hard to breach. This is a large part of craft's appeal. It keeps us from having to face our readers or ourselves too directly. One reason we're so fascinated by writing techniques is that they promise to help us tap-dance elegantly around what we really have to say. That's also why overly polished writing can be so tedious. Fashioning a mask from elegant words not only makes for bad writing but is futile anyway. "Everybody knows it's a mask," said Katherine Anne Porter, "and sooner or later you must show yourself as someone who could not afford to show himself, and so created something to hide behind."

Mastery of craft can be the very tool that allows a writer

to avoid verities. I'd much rather read an inelegant, honest writer than a glib, evasive one.

In the midst of debate about whether gays should be allowed to serve in the military, a security guard, a former marine named Charles W. Redd, Jr., wrote:

> I recently returned from a trip I only seem to be able to take every 10 years, to visit two of the best friends I've ever had. My reason for not being able to make this trip really has nothing to do with a lack of funds or time; it's just that the last time I saw these two dear friends they were both sprawled in red mud, lifeless and torn apart by angry pieces of metal.
>
> For years I had nightmares about these two brothers. One was from the deep South and one from the ghettos of Philly. We became very close to each other. Francis, from Birmingham, Ala., had saved my life in an ambush, for which he received the Bronze Star. But the shock of my life came when I found out he was gay.
>
> The topic came up in a conversation the night before he was killed on Hill 881. He was killed by a failure of his weapon; that failure due most likely to some straight butthead in the United States sending inferior ammo to Vietnam. The night be-fore he was killed, Douglas and I toasted Francis as one of the straightest brothers we had met.
>
> There had never been anything to hint that Francis was gay. He didn't molest babies. He never tried to get into my bunk. I never felt him looking at me when we showered. He was a

Marine—a good Marine who fought and died
for his country. . . .

I don't understand homosexuality, but I don't
fear it either. So-called straight people worry me
more. If gay people want the right to serve and
die for America, let them.

The more I read, and write, the more convinced I am that
good writing has less to do with acquired technique than
with inner conviction. The assurance that you have something to say that the world needs to hear counts for more than
literary skill. Those writers who hold their readers' attention
are the ones who grab them by the lapel and say, "You've *got*
to listen to what I'm about to tell you." It's hard to be that
passionate. It means you must put your whole poke on the
table. Yet this very go-for-broke quality grabs and holds a
reader far more surely than any mastery of technique.

I once went into a Delaware school district to solicit
writing by students about their fathers. The worst essays I
got were typed neatly on bond paper, had few punctuation
errors, and displayed the writers' command of language.
Some were placed neatly in plastic sleeves. The writing I
liked best came to me on lined notebook paper, often with
a fringe at the edge where it had been torn from a binder.
Pencil was the tool most often used to produce this writing.
It was usually filled with errors of spelling, grammar, and
punctuation. And some of it knocked me out. Here are two
examples, the first from an eleven-year-old boy, the second
from one of sixteen.

I think my father is the best father in the whole
world. He is forty-one years old. When I was

little he used to pick me up—so far that my head would touch the ceiling. Now I'm too old so he can't pick me up anymore. And also because he had an operation on his back. Dad used to take me to the rifle range a lot of times. Now he don't take me out so often. Once in a while I kid him about the little gray hairs on his chest. He can still put his arms around me.

This story is about my father. He is just a normal, old-fashioned father. What I mean by old-fashioned is that when we are at the supper table you have to ask if you can have more bread and butter. And if you don't ask he'll smack you over the knuckles with a butter knife.

His strictest rule is not to get into trouble and not to give my mother a big mouth. If I give my mom a big mouth that night I have to either do some fast talking or fast running. Many times I dove under the bed to get away from him or behind the couch. And he pulled me out by my pants and beat the shit out of me. But he's my father and I respect him as a father. He's a full-blooded Irishman with a mean temper. But he's not mean all the time, just when I do something wrong he gets mad. For my sixteenth birthday he got me a car, then two months later I got into an accident and had to junk my car. After they hauled it away he bought me another one.

My dad is almost 54 now and I think that in his family everybody passed on at about 60–65. But he's been working about 12 hours a day since he

was 16 and when he dies I will never hold a
grudge against him.

What I like most about such writing is that its authors are
less concerned about "writing" than with saying what's on
their mind and not worrying about how it sounds. As a
result theirs sounds best of all. I always like to get such
writing in a class because it encourages others—"stylish"
writers in particular—to be bolder. That's also why I prefer
to have no prerequisites for my classes. Since you never
know where good writing will come from, I'd rather take
whoever walks through the door. A night school course I
taught, whose members ranged in age from thirteen to
seventy-six, included one of my best students ever. Tina
was a go-go dancer with a ninth-grade education who
wandered into my writing class because the one on ESP was
filled. Her classmates always paid rapt attention when Tina
read a story she'd written. One was about a topless dancer
contemplating suicide as she danced, wondering how the
audience would react. Another portrayed a woman trying
to cope with a boyfriend who had returned from Vietnam
strung out on heroin. A third story depicted a woman
having her first lesbian affair. Even though her paper rattled
as she gripped the page, Tina read these stories aloud. She
showed us what I've seen so many times: that the fear of
writing *can* be confronted, can be transcended, and—best
of all—can be harnessed and put to work.

6

Putting Fear to Work

> Anxiety is the essential condition
> of intellectual and artistic
> creation and everything that is
> finest in human history.
> —*Charles Frankel*

At a party she hosted, Joan Didion felt suffocated by the crowd. Didion thought about seeking refuge in the bathroom or perhaps taking a walk. Instead she went to her office and sat before the typewriter. This restored her equilibrium. "I'm much more comfortable dealing with a typewriter than with talking," Didion once said. "I can't even finish sentences when I'm talking. In the middle, I guess I decide it's not a very good sentence and I just stop."

Joan Didion has always portrayed herself as catatonically shy. Those who interview the essayist-novelist confirm this self-assessment. Didion was less than a "virtuoso conversationalist," one observed drily. After a long silence while she struggled to answer an interviewer's question, Didion finally admitted, "Sometimes I think I can't think at all unless I'm behind my typewriter. Like now I'm just recording sensory impressions, the light bouncing off the floor, your tapestry bag."

As a child, Didion suffered from a smorgasbord of fears. These ranged from ski lifts through snakes to stories in comic books. As an adult, she remained anxious but with less certainty about what was scaring her. Didion has said that one reason she writes is to identify her fears and come to terms with them. The author compared this process to one in which a doctor gets a child to tell stories, then uses these stories to determine what's bothering that child. "Well, a novel is just a story," said Didion. "You work things out in the stories you tell."

In the process of working things out, Didion has written some unusually vibrant prose. James Dickey once called her the best woman stylist writing in English. Far from being hobbled by anxiety, Didion made it into an art form. Those who praise Joan Didion's writing invariably note the tone of controlled panic that lifts it off the page. Gloria Steinem paid tribute to her "finely observed terror in the ordinary." Alfred Kazin praised the powerful "sense of fright" her writing conveyed. Added Kazin, "She writes about her panics with a deliberation that is not merely disarming but that always makes a point."

A Taste for Fear

Until now we've discussed fear as something that can be tolerated, confronted, and made less ominous. Now let's go farther and look at fear as not just an incidental but an *invaluable* part of the writing process.

It's understandable to assume that good writing happens despite anxiety, that the best writers are those who have mastered their fears. It could be the other way around. Far from being fearless, authors tend to be anxious people who are duking it out with their anxieties on the page. They don't write *despite* their fear but *because* of it. They want to wrestle that alligator. Though few make an art form of anxiety to the degree that a Didion has, writers tend to have a taste for fear. "I usually write about things that frighten me," agreed Israeli author David Grossman. "Otherwise, what's the point?" Like Grossman, many authors write to confront their own fears. In the process, they hope to understand them better and perhaps defuse their power. Rosellen Brown—who said she writes novels with a sense of "sheer terror"—admitted to the almost superstitious hope that converting her worst fears into fiction might keep them from actually happening.

A writer's fears are never "conquered." Nor should they be. Were an antidote discovered to literary anxiety, writers would be deprived of a powerful ally. When anxious, I'm also sharp: alert, observant, sometimes even witty. Fear energizes me. At my ease—with family, say—I'm prone to mumble, ramble, repeat myself, look at the floor, and feel little need to be funny. Whatever charm I possess is anxiety-driven. When meeting someone new, I try to make good eye contact, express my thoughts clearly, and stay alert for opportunities to entertain. The same thing is true when I'm addressing readers. Catherine Drinker Bowen said that this was exactly why she liked writers to be afraid. "They can show their fear by a noble defiance in their work or by a beguiling charm and grace in seeking to win their public," explained Bowen. "At least those fearful ones are not writing for themselves alone. They are seeking to communicate, and their fear is proof of it."

Fear is never enjoyable. But nerves are part of the writing process, perhaps even an essential part. That's what most working writers eventually come to accept. Anxiety is always there; a daffy old uncle in the attic who stomps about, rattles his chains, and makes a ruckus. One may not like working to the tune of rattling chains, but in time it comes to feel normal. The uncle causing a commotion can even be brought down from the attic and made to earn his keep.

Over time, writers learn how to manipulate fear, bargain with it, harness its power. It's important here to distinguish between toxic and nutritious anxiety. One blocks, the other arouses. Fortunately, inhibiting fear can be converted into energizing fear. To do this, however, one must engage anxiety and convert it into exhilaration. That's what E. B. White discovered. For all of his page fright, White found that "a blank sheet of paper holds the greatest excitement there is for me. . . . It holds all the hope there is, all fears."

Fear invariably precedes excitement. We all knew that when we were six. Relearning this lesson puts writing fears in a new light. It's not fear's presence or intensity or the apparent bravado of writers that determines their ability to write in the face of anxiety. Rather it's the approach they take toward fear.

When psychologist Thomas McKain of Washington, D.C., studied high- and low-anxiety writers for his Ph.D. thesis, one message stood out: it wasn't the degree of anxiety that crippled an ability to write so much as the attitude subjects had about that anxiety. Those who fell victim to their fears were the ones who saw only peril in anxiety. Writers who saw challenge there too had much less difficulty recording their thoughts on paper.

Faced with danger, we all recoil. That's natural. The unanswered question is, What do we do next? If the danger stems from a risk we'd like to take, do we turn toward that risk or away from it? Critic Kenneth Burke thought great artists saw opportunity in anxious experiences that most people found merely menacing. Argentine novelist Luisa Valenzuela said that when afraid she felt most alive, best able to write with her whole body. This was a lesson she learned early. "I was the kind of child who always poked around wherever there was fear," said Valenzuela, "to see what kind of a creature fear was."

As this perspective suggests, the seeds of a solution to writing anxiety lie within the problem itself. Rather, within our ability not to regard this anxiety as a "problem." The very best writing grows out of our fears. Put another way, for a writer, fear is nothing to be afraid of.

Counterphobia

Just before she was appointed America's poet laureate, Rita Dove published her first novel, *Through the Ivory Gate*. Dove had wanted to write this book for years but kept putting it off. What finally turned the tide was her very anxiety about doing so. "My fear of writing a novel was simply due to the fact that I hadn't done it before," explained Dove, "and part of the challenge was to go ahead and do it just because I wanted to overcome my fear."

History books bulge with accounts of those who excelled at a activity they undertook because it scared them. The stammering, bullied young Winston Churchill turned himself into a fierce warrior and eloquent orator. James Earl Jones started acting to overcome a stutter so severe that it left him virtually mute. Wire walker Philippe Petit—who once spent an hour walking on a cable strung between the World Trade Center's twin towers, 1,350 feet above the ground— told me that he suffered from a lifelong fear of heights. Similarly, Erica Jong has said the best things that happened to her resulted from a willingness to do what scared her most. Writing *Fear of Flying*, for example—even though she was sure her family would disown her and her husband evict her—to Jong was "a kind of counterphobic performance."

Psychoanalyst Otto Fenichel originated the concept of counterphobia. Counterphobics basically try to inoculate themselves against anxiety by engaging in activities that scare them. Fenichel saw a convergence of daredevils and artists in their childlike fascination with fear. Picasso—who called painting a means of "giving form to our terrors as well as our desires"—was a classic example. So was Hemingway, who struggled throughout his life to tame inner fears by proving outer courage. "I was a very fearful child," admitted Jessamyn West, another counterphobic, "and for this reason had constantly to be battling my fears by doing what frightened me most."

The Secret Weapon

It's startling to discover how timid some very bold writers were in person. James Joyce, for example, spent his life terrorized by dogs, rats, and claps of thunder. Emily Dickinson rarely left her parents' home. Proust sealed out the world beyond his study with cork-lined walls. How can such meek and mild authors dare to write at all, let alone well? In fact, the two may be connected. Their very timidity makes them write as if their lives depended on it. A backs-to-the-wall sensibility gives intensity to the words of a White, a Didion, and a Raymond Chandler.

Chandler was a gripping stylist. He set such a standard for mystery writers that three and a half decades after his death, Chandler's successors are still compared to him. None has ever matched the edgy mood of a good Raymond Chandler novel or story. Their author—who was the sole survivor of his World War I platoon—puzzled over the fact that his many imitators couldn't bring magic to a scene the way he could. "Very likely they write better mysteries than I do," Chandler conceded, "but their words don't get up and walk. Mine do, although it is embarrassing to admit it."

> There was a desert wind blowing that night. It was one of those hot dry Santa Anas that come down through the mountain passes and curl your hair and make your nerves jump and your skin itch. On nights like that every booze party ends in a fight. Meek little wives feel the edge of the carving knife and study their husbands' necks. Anything can happen.

The British author finally concluded that what made his work so singular was its "smell of fear." Despite his heroism in the war, Chandler was almost pathologically shy. "Courage is a strange thing," he once wrote, "one can never be sure of it. As a platoon commander very many years ago I never seemed to be afraid, and yet I have been afraid of the most insignificant risks." There were times when Chandler could complete a project only after calming his nerves with liberal doses of alcohol. Yet the more of a shambles Chandler's personal life became, the better his writing grew. Biographer Frank MacShane concluded that the two were probably connected: that Chandler needed the petrol of anxiety to fuel his literary engine.

Creative people of all kinds use anxiety as an energy source. They hone the blade of their work against fear's strop until it gets a keen, sharp edge. Gripping writing results from intensity, and intensity is the flip side of fear. Some writers don't feel they're getting anywhere until anxiety kicks in. "I'm very excited because it scares the living daylights out of me," Paul Auster once said about a novel he was writing. "Every time I come to work on it, I'm scared. I think maybe that's a good sign."

Like a daredevil's audience, readers sense when a writer feels in jeopardy and pay close attention. Daring is always more riveting than skill. Any juggler knows that the real crowd pleaser isn't his hardest task, such as keeping five balls in the air. The biggest oohs and ahhs are reserved for feats that look as though they could maim him: juggling three lit torches, say, or that many sharp machetes. Bold writers have the same relationship to readers that a juggler has to his crowd. When they seem about to catch an errant machete by the blade, their readers stay glued to the page.

There are reasons for the appeal of bold writing that go beyond the fascination of watching authors in danger of breaking their literary necks. Good writing is honest, alive. The more honest and alive our writing, the more we show ourselves. The more we show ourselves, the greater danger we're in. The greater danger we're in, the more scared we are. Hence fear is a marker on the path toward good writing. "When you stiffen," said Toni Morrison of anxious moments while writing a novel, "you know that whatever

you stiffen about is very important. The stuff is important,
the fear itself is information."

This is the benign side of the courage to write. It's not all
hunker down, grit your teeth, and stiffen your upper lip.
The child who pleads "Scare me again, Daddy. Scare me
again!" knows something most adults have forgotten: how
thrilling fear can be. A writer aroused by terror is more
likely to arouse the reader. As James M. Cain once observed, writing that doesn't keep the writer up at night
won't keep the reader up either.

A young mother in one class of mine held her classmates
spellbound as she read a portrait of a pederast from the
pederast's point of view. The man Karen described cruised
suburban streets much like her own until he spotted a
susceptible-looking young girl. The child molester lured
this girl into his car by saying her mother had asked him to
drive her home. He then enticed her into a "touching
game," involving the crotch of his pants. The author described this game in unflinching detail. Though obviously
confronting a primordial fear (she kept having to stop and
catch her breath while reading it aloud), Karen dealt with
her fear by writing about it. To do this, she had to explore
her own thoughts and fears about pederasts, then dare to tell
us what she discovered. Karen's sketch was the best piece of
writing we got in that class, the only one to which everyone
gave one hundred percent of their attention.

It's safe to assume that readers are dealing with fears of
their own. They can sniff out the writer who is sharing this
ride, perhaps a little more boldly than they are. Reading the
work of anxious, courageous writers makes them feel less
alone. This is yet another way that anxiety can help writing:
it connects author and reader.

An interviewer once asked Robert Stone if the strange and frightening things he wrote about were things he feared himself. "It's a commonplace idea, isn't it, to be drawn to the things you fear," responded Stone. But he didn't see this as a problem. To the contrary, said Stone, "The reader and I will consider how strange and frightening things are and we will laugh about it, having no other alternative, and thus transcend it and assert the positive part of our humanity and perhaps make it less fearsome. . . . I want to share that sense of the terrifying nature of things with my hypothetical reader and, as a result of our sharing it, produce a positive experience that gives rise to hope and transcendence. That's what I'm trying to do."

Wonderfully Concentrated Minds

While doing research for a book on risk taking (*Chancing It: Why We Take Risks*), I hung around several comedy clubs. Invariably those about to go on stage—regardless of how many times they'd done so previously—were nearly catatonic with fear. It was hard to see how they could possibly face an audience. But all did, every one of them, instantly converting their nerves into nervous energy when faced with a roomful of faces. ("Hi, how ya doin' out there? Where ya from? Jersey? I spent a week in Jersey one day.")

The frantic, wired energy of most comedians onstage grows directly from the black terror they experience while waiting to go on. Writing is a form of performance. Page fright, like stage fright, can be turned into focus. What's good about stage fright, said actress Jeanne Moreau, "is that it's transformed into concentration as soon as you're working."

Fear does concentrate the mind wonderfully. Like actors, athletes accept this out of hand. A batter who strikes out or a goalkeeper who lets a soccer ball into the net will often explain, "I wasn't scared enough." Boxing manager Cus D'Amato told his fighters, "Fear is your best friend." By this, D'Amato meant that boxers who weren't afraid let their attention wander. A fighter with anything on his mind other than the man trying to knock him out soon found himself on the floor looking up at another man in a bow tie counting to ten. "They manipulate fear," said former light-heavyweight champion José Torres of great boxers. "They use fear as the best and only developer of superlative sense of anticipation. They convert panic and anxiety—two of the negative components of fear—into alertness and meticulous vigilance. Once mastered, fear becomes the trusted and devoted watchful eye of champions."

The same thing is true of writers. Concentration is as much the coin of their realm as it is of athletes' and actors'. A tranquil writer can have trouble staying focused on the task at hand. Those who convert fear into focus have a potent weapon in their arsenal. Writers who are afraid of a manuscript but work on it anyway will give that work the same degree of concentration that they'd pay to a forest fire whose heat has begun to sear their skin.

Details, Details

If writers and writing teachers agree on one point, it's the need for *detail* to lift words off the page. Detail is a product of intense concentration and observation. Yet it's hard to observe the world too intensely when one feels complacent. Attention wanders. There's dinner to plan, plumbers to call, clothes to pick up at the cleaners. Anxious writers are less prone to let their minds drift. They pay attention to the details of the world around them as if their very existence depended on it.

Joan Didion has compared her obsession with life's ephemera to that of a schizophrenic. Many consider this attention to detail Didion's strongest quality as a writer. Her ability to record telling minutiae is a product not just of Joan Didion's anxious alertness but of her willingness to go to scary places. This is how she described a single hour spent in the Panama airport on her way to an unsettling research trip for her novel *A Book of Common Prayer.* "I can still feel the hot air when I step off the plane, can see the heat already rising off the tarmac at 6 A.M. I can feel my skirt damp and wrinkled on my legs. I can feel the asphalt stick to my sandals. I remember the big tail of a Pan American plane floating motionless down at the end of the tarmac. I remember the sound of a slot machine in the waiting room."

The awareness promoted by anxiety is far more valuable to a writer than any report of anxiety itself. Saying that anxious writers can be better writers doesn't mean they have to be confessional. After being assigned to describe a personal experience, a high school student I taught called me at home to ask if that meant he had to write something "personal." He didn't like to reveal himself, the boy said. If I insisted on it, he'd drop the course. In a long conversation I explained to him that it wasn't personal revelation I was looking for as much as the *immediacy* of a personal experience that was a little anxious. In response this student wrote an excellent sketch about sledding down a hill when he was five, feeling little daggers of snow pierce his nose, mouth, and eyes.

When assigned to write about an immediate sensory experience, another student of mine—a college freshman who kept threatening to bolt the class because she was so frightened—described a stream of sensation set off by a few minutes spent in the school cafeteria:

> I pick two slices of lemon from a community bowl. The first is thin. I squeeze the lemon between both hands with my thumbs and forefingers. I squeeze a soggy dish rag. My mouth secretes saliva. I cut my finger and blood oozes to the surface of my skin. The juice seeps into my cuticles. I chew a piece of candy with a remaining piece of tin foil.
>
> The second lemon slice is thick. The skin is bumpy and moist. I stroke the neck of a frog. The scent is sweet. I smell the lupine. The slice is ripe and filled with juice. I see a tick that is fat and filled with blood. I squeeze the lemon between both hands with my thumbs and forefingers. I smash a tick with my shoe. The juice squirts. The blood squishes out. The seeds hit the edge of the glass. Small pieces of gravel often strike the windshield of a moving car.

Such attention to detail is usually a product of anxiety. While studying risk taking, I was struck by the specificity with which subjects recalled moments when they felt in danger. At a reunion of Pearl Harbor survivors, one veteran said he could still remember the name of a book he was reading beneath the shade of a tarp on the U.S.S. *Honolulu* that languid Sunday morning in 1941 (*Rain in the Doorway*), its author (Thorne Smith), and the color of its cover (green). Others recalled markings on planes come to bomb them and even the expression on the faces of their pilots.

Fear flushes clogged pores of perception. Ears listening for the crunch of bears' paws, eyes scanning the horizon for enemy soldiers, and noses sniffing the air for the smell of fire have heightened awareness. Presumably such alertness helped us survive in a world of marauding mastodons and attacking enemy tribes. It can also make for vivid prose.

> It seemed to the youth that he saw everything. Each blade of green grass was bold and clear. He thought that he was aware of every change in the thin, transparent vapor that floated idly in sheets. The brown or gray trunks of the trees showed each roughness of their surfaces. . . . His mind took a mechanical but firm impression, so that afterwards everything was pictured and explained to him, save why he himself was there.

This description of a soldier about to go into battle, from *The Red Badge of Courage* by Stephen Crane, suggests the partnership between fear and heightened perception. There may be a neurochemical explanation for that partnership. Psychologists call vividly recalled anxious moments "flashbulb memories." Intense stress illuminates everything in sight when we feel frightened. It seems that brain chemicals stimulated by fear fix even minute details of anxious settings in our memory. Flashbulb memories can range from the dress we were wearing when John Kennedy died to both names of our high school classmates. Six years after she survived a train accident, writer Jena Heath said, "I remember every detail of my rescuer's face. I can taste how good his neighbor's coffee felt sliding down my throat."

Bad days are easier to write about than good days. They make a much bigger impression. Most of those alive at the time remember what they were doing on November 22, 1963, after hearing that John Kennedy was killed. But who remembers what happened on November 21? "Listen the next time your find yourself describing an auto accident . . . or hearing a similar trauma described," suggested Susan Shaughnessy in her book *Walking on Alligators*. "You'll notice the vigor and economy of the language. There are no frills—just simple, compelling narrative."

Consider the following piece of writing:

> In a few minutes Mom and Dad are going out to eat. She's got on a long-sleeved yellow dress, black fish-net nylons and black heels. When she doesn't notice, Dad looks at her. Then he rests his head on the back of the red chair and closes his eyes.
>
> Last night Bob brought me home at twelve o'clock. We had been wrestling and playing tag on the grass in the back of Sangren. We were still laughing when he let me out of the car. I pinched his buns and then he messed up my hair. We gave each other a noisy kiss under our five-watt porch light, and he left.
>
> Mom and Dad were still up. I was relieved because I thought we might have wakened them.

I started to go upstairs when Dad asked me to wait. I put my books down and sat at the desk. Mom's face was tight and her freckles were little red spots. Dad kept puffing on his pipe. He began, "Your mother and I have decided to get a divorce. But even though I'm leaving, remember you're still my daughter and you always will be."

Then he started to cry. Mom and I were crying too. I ran over and put my arms around him. His tears felt hot on my cheek. Then he said, "Go to your mother. She feels bad too."

He left tonight—to his little apartment on Copper Street. Mom helped him move, and she cried when she saw it. The bedroom is lavender with a purple bedspread. The furniture looks like Antique Barn. A big crack runs up and down the door. When he left, he took a lamp, four glasses, and an ash tray.

That sketch was written by a college freshman assigned to write extemporaneously for twenty minutes. The student's obvious distress—raw and fresh—gives her words power. Their tone of controlled panic demands that we pay attention. Such prose is powerful precisely because it is less concerned with "writing" as such than with communicating strong feeling through revealing detail and unadorned words. Ken Macrorie, the professor who got this assignment, later commented, "Using no chart or program for recording pertinent details, this writer had found her way."

So did a high school senior in Ohio who began an essay by recalling the most shocking thing that ever happened to her, her mother's death from pneumonia when she was seven:

> When they first told me, it didn't seem real, and I didn't know what was going on. My thoughts raced as I cried; I thought about the stormy nights when she comforted me. I thought of the grape bubble gum she would buy me every time she went to the store. Sometimes when she used to tell us to go to bed, my brother and I would sit on the steps and watch TV from a distance . . .
>
> Until my mother died, I hadn't been too close to my father. But after her death, I clung to him. I was just like a little shadow to him. I would follow him around and wait for him to come home so I could be near him . . .
>
> Then, when I was 12, the second-most shocking thing in my life happened. I was in school (just like I had been when I learned about my mother's death) when the school secretary came and talked to my teacher. I was taken to the office where my older brother waited to take me home.
>
> It was a familiar feeling. While in the back seat of the car, I laid my head down and began to cry silently. I knew that even though he hadn't been sick, my father had died. I could feel it.
>
> We arrived at our apartment, where I last saw my dad that morning. Before they closed the front door, my emotions took over. The tears rolled down my face.
>
> My brother told us that my father had been in

a car accident. I tried so hard to hold it in, but I let go of everything that had built up all the way from school. I cried the rest of the day, on and off—my nose was sore, my eyes swollen and my feelings crushed. I loved my father . . .

The thought of a 12 year-old without any parents still haunts me. After my parents died, things were not the same.

Kids were afraid to talk to me; they asked stupid questions and whispered behind my back. My teachers gave me extra attention that I didn't want.

Opening Pores

John Berryman thought the luckiest artists were those who endured terrible ordeals that didn't actually kill them. We all won't be that lucky. But to break the shackles of inhibition, we do sometimes need a bit of crisis, a dash of calamity. That's why the rich loam of adolescence—a time of constant crisis and ceaseless calamity—beckons writers to till and retill youthful memories; "just like a criminal goes back to the place of his crime," said Isaac Bashevis Singer. John Updike thought little happened to the writer after the age of twenty that was worth writing about. Willa Cather put the cutoff at fifteen, Ignazio Silone at twelve. "Many writers do little else but sit in small rooms recalling the real world," noted Annie Dillard. "This explains why so many books describe the author's childhood. A writer's childhood may well have been the occasion of his only firsthand experience."

In *Through the Ivory Gate*, the novel she wrote because it

scared her, Rita Dove described a girl named Virginia who was the only black majorette in her largely white high school. The experience makes Virginia painfully aware of the difference between herself and her fellow majorettes.

> They tried to mold their bodies to the *Vogue* standard, glamorous in their long straight hair and sharp noses, their peach-colored chemises and sheer nylons. Whenever they changed into their uniforms for pep assembly, Virginia peeked at their flowered bikini panties and lacy bras. She had never seen such extravagance, and she tried not to stare when they stripped off these very same undergarments after assembly and washed up at the sinks, chatting as if it were the most natural thing in the world.

Most of us lose our ability to observe the world this directly along with our roller skates and baseball gloves. The older we grow, the harder it gets to see our surroundings in detail. This has less to do with declining eyesight than with the security zones so many of us create to protect ourselves from surprises. The ability to muffle anxiety feels like a perk of adulthood. We cut a Faustian deal: in return for not being so anxious all the time, we agree to tune down our whole nervous system. As a result, our powers of observation decline along with our sense of smell, taste, and hearing. This is partly a function of dulled senses, partly due to the fact that we're seeing so little that's surprising. This perk poses a problem for writers. How can they keep their perceptions fresh in the face of advancing maturity?

Some feel that the best way to punch up their prose is to

place themselves in jeopardy. Writers such as Oriana Fallaci, Ernest Hemingway, and Graham Greene did this by chasing wars. (When locals told him that they wished he could have seen their country at peace, Greene would think, "but all that interests me here is your war.") Others climb mountains or explore caverns. Still more explore inner caves. They have affairs, get therapy, dare their unconscious to surface.

Psychic risks can be harder to take than those that merely threaten one's physical well-being. When studying risk taking, I wanted to take a turn as a stand-up comedian but didn't. Although given the opportunity, I found the prospect of telling jokes to a roomful of faces that might not laugh too scary by half. Instead I joined a rock climbing expedition. In the process, I learned something about the partnership of fear and awareness. I discovered that looking for fingernail holds while struggling up a sheer seventy-foot wall of granite promotes a remarkable consciousness of one's immediate surroundings. This consciousness got translated into a nifty piece of writing about my expedition.

Pushing our envelope adds tingle to writing. It forces us to work along our nerve endings. Literary risk taking needn't involve daredevilry. I sometimes try to tweak the perceptions of students by simply taking them into unfamiliar settings. We've gone on winter camping expeditions, visited nontourist's Tijuana, and toured unfamiliar sections of our own towns in search of fresh observations. When assigned to visit a new setting, one young woman—who grew up within thirty miles of Philadelphia—took her first trip to that city. There she chatted with locals, some of whom were homeless, and returned to write an evocative description of her adventure.

Such expeditions have sometimes produced surprising results. By taking one class to Tijuana, I'd hoped to get reports about the smell of tortillas frying, the sound of salsa music blaring, the sight of stores packed with locals buying Nikes and Pepsi-Cola. The best essay of all, however, was one man's flight of fantasy about Tijuana's sidewalks parting to let him fall into a dungeon below. There, a huge Tijuanan—stripped to the waist—banged a gong and berated the writer-tourist for presuming to ogle him and his countrymen.

Most writers don't need to prime the pump of their anxieties. Writing is anxious enough. Fear is as much a part of the writing process as periods and commas. It can't be eradicated and shouldn't be. Within reason, being frightened keeps the writer alert. "As much as there is joy in writing," said novelist Robert Cormier, "there's always the little bit of terror to keep you on edge, on your toes."

Even though that bit of terror can be invaluable to writers, it can't always be confronted head-on. That's why, as I'll discuss in the next chapter, experienced writers develop elaborate tactics to manipulate fear so they can keep writing.

7

Should You Write in the Nude?

> Any the smallest alteration
> of my silent daily habits
> produces anarchy in me.
> —*Thomas Carlyle*

A friend of mine named Lorraine left an insurance company to become a writer. After a few days, Lorraine called to get some pointers about her new career. "You've been writing for a few years, right?" she began.

"Right," I answered.

"Well, I have a very important question to ask you."

"Yes?"

"Do you get dressed in the morning or what?"

. . .

Early in his career, John Cheever put on a business suit, then went from his apartment to a room in the basement where he hung his suit on a hanger and wrote in his underwear. Victor Hugo's servant took away his clothes for the duration of the author's writing day. James Whitcomb Riley had a friend lock him in a hotel room without clothes so that he couldn't go out for a drink until he had finished writing. Jessamyn West wrote in bed without getting dressed for what she thought were two compelling reasons: "One, you have on your nightgown or pajamas and can't go running to the door at the knock of strangers. Also, once you're up and dressed, you see ten thousand things that need doing."

Whether to dress up, down, or not at all is a major concern of working writers. While conducting an informal poll on writers' sartorial habits, I interrupted one friend's work to ask if she dressed to write. The blush racing unmistakably through the phone lines told me she didn't. Another colleague said she wouldn't dare don more than a bathrobe while writing because doing so would make it possible to step out for a carton of milk or return a book to the library. A surprising number of writers belong to the Bathrobe School. When he first started writing, John McPhee not only worked in his bathrobe but tied its sash to the arms of his chair to keep from even thinking about leaving. William Maxwell wrote novels while wearing a bathrobe and pajamas as a visual warning not to disturb him until he got dressed. Novelist Hope Dahle Jordan wouldn't shed her robe until she'd written five hundred acceptable words. "That is the only way to get a book finished," she contended. "For as long as I stay in my blue bathrobe I stay at my typewriter."

Other writers look down on this school. "You can't hang around in your bathrobe and slop around the house all day," argued novelist Anne Bernays. "In order to really crank it up you need to get dressed and put on your shoes and act as if you're going to an office to work." Benjamin Disraeli wrote novels while dressed in evening clothes. Keats said of his typical workday: "I rouse myself, wash and put on a clean shirt . . . in fact adonise as if I were going out—then all clean and comfortable I sit down to write."

My own approach is closer to that of Bernays-Disraeli-Keats than the Bathrobe School. I dress to write. Casually, but I dress. My biggest indulgence is to work barefoot at times or in slippers during the winter. Even this concerns me. First I'll work in slippers. Then maybe just a bathrobe. After that, perhaps underwear alone. This might lead me to ask: Why get out of bed at all? Why write, for that matter? Reviewing this checklist motivates me to pull on a pair of pants and button up a shirt.

What's more interesting than the dress habits of writers per se is the rationale behind them. Whether one wears a bathrobe, a tux, or nothing at all has little to do with the quality of one's words. But it can have everything to do with one's ability to write in the first place. Their choice of working attire (or lack thereof) is one among many tactics writers devise to buck up their nerve so they can confront the blank page and fill it with words.

The Tactical Writer

Most writers work alone. Over time, they come to feel like a lone astronaut in a small spaceship. Pebbles thrown by friends sometimes clatter on their window. Occasionally their agent rattles the doorknob. Or an editor whistles through the keyhole. But with such exceptions, writers must get themselves from one day to the next. Without the routines of an office, lone workers develop quirky work habits. Deprived of a boss or coworkers to apply the lash, they learn how to apply their own. As creative people, writers come up with imaginative ways to goose themselves, summon the muse, and avoid stepping out for a newspaper. Robert Graves found that surrounding himself with man-made objects—wooden figurines, porcelain clown heads, books printed by hand—improved his spiritual atmosphere. California poet Joaquin Miller had sprinklers installed above his home because he could only compose poetry to the sound of rain on the roof. Henrik Ibsen hung a picture of August Strindberg over his desk. "He is my mortal enemy and shall hang there and watch while I write!" explained Ibsen.

The most inventive strategist of all was Friedrich Schiller. Schiller kept red curtains drawn in his study because he thought that the glow of sunlight soaking through them stimulated his imagination. Sometimes the playwright immersed his bare feet in cold water to stay alert. He also kept rotten apples in a deskside cupboard. When visiting Schiller, Goethe was overpowered by their odor. He asked Schiller's wife why the spoiled fruit was there. She explained that her husband thought its putrid smell aroused him, and that he couldn't work without it.

Whatever it takes. All writers develop their own methods to approach the page. "Writing is so personal, so profoundly and terribly personal," said Elie Wiesel. "Your entire personality goes into every word. The hesitation between one word and another is filled with many centuries, much space. And you deal with it one way, because of what you are, and somebody else deals with it another way. There are no rules. Even technically, some writers need all kinds of idiosyncrasies. One took a wet cloth to his forehead; another had to get drunk; a third had to take drugs; Hemingway stood, another was sitting, another was lying.

Would you say that there are precepts that you have to sit or lie?"

Apparently not. Like Hemingway, Virginia Woolf, Lewis Carroll, and Günter Grass worked standing up. The six-foot-six-inch Thomas Wolfe sometimes wrote using the top of his refrigerator as a desk. Robert Browning wore holes in Elizabeth Barrett's carpet as he shuffled about composing poems. Wallace Stevens composed poetry while walking to work every day at a Hartford insurance company. Brendan Gill described how his sister stood at a window of her Hartford home one morning and observed Stevens passing by:

> As she watched, he slowed down, came to a stop, rocked in place for a moment or two, took a step backward, hesitated, then strode confidently forward—left, right, left, right—on his way to work. It was obvious to her that Stevens had gone back over a phrase, dropped an unsatisfactory word, inserted a superior one, and proceeded to the next line of the poem he was making.

Unlike the vertical writers, many assume Jessamyn West's posture and work in bed. Reclining writers have included Mark Twain, Truman Capote, Eudora Welty, and Edith Wharton. While writing *Sophie's Choice*, William Styron kept a bed by his desk where he often lay "in supine concentration or supine despair." When told of this tactic, Mary Gordon was astonished. "Bed is the devil," said Gordon. "When I lie down, I go to sleep."

Rituals

Why do writers develop such odd work habits? The obvious answer is that they're odd people. But I think there's a more basic reason for their eccentric working styles. These techniques play an important anxiety-easing role that is ill appreciated even by those who employ them. William Gass thought what really motivated his colleagues' peculiar ways was insecurity about going into the void. "Writers have certain compulsions, certain ordering habits, which are part of the book only in the sense that they make its writing possible," explained Gass. "Psychologically these games are necessary. Every writer plays them, though what they are varies a good deal."

What they really are, of course, are rites. Ritualized behavior is common among those who do dangerous work. Mine-disposal experts, for example, temper their fear of being blown to bits by developing superstitious routines. One eats the same food every day. Another dresses a certain way each morning. A third recites mantras while traveling to and from minefields. Writers also confront danger's demons in ceremonial ways. "The variations are infinite," said novelist John Edgar Wideman, "but each writer knows his or her version of the preparatory ritual must be exactly duplicated if writing is to begin, prosper." Hemingway sharpened twenty pencils before starting to write. Isabel Allende lit a candle for dead relatives. Jack Kerouac began his nightly writing stints on his knees in prayer, then wrote by candlelight. "It's like the habit of Catholics going into water," said Nobel laureate Derek Walcott of such ceremonies; "you cross yourself before you go in. Any serious attempt to try to do something worthwhile is ritualistic."

Totems

Many writers attach great importance to the tools of their craft. Such tools vary, but not the conviction with which their use is defended. Passionate views about what is and isn't a proper writing implement have less to do with the physical act of getting words on paper than with placating the gods. Tools are totems, an important weapon in the fight against fear. John Barth drafted his novels with a fountain pen not only because he preferred its feel but because he found composing on a typewriter too inhibiting. "The idea of typing out first drafts," explained Barth, "where each letter is physically separated by a little space from the next letter, I find a paralyzing notion." Barth's fellow Baltimorean Anne Tyler also used a fountain pen, finding that pushing its nib across paper helped get her imagination in gear. Robert Graves preferred the feel of a steel-nib pen that had to be dipped in a pot of ink.

Late in his career, Pablo Neruda broke a finger and could no longer type. Of necessity, he went back to composing poems with a pen. The change proved felicitous. When written by hand, Neruda found, his poetry was "more sensitive, its plastic forms could change more easily." Poets especially seem to feel more connected to words that flow directly through their fingers. Elizabeth Bishop said she could compose prose on a typewriter, but not poetry. She wrote verse by hand. Rilke circulated handwritten copies of his poems because he wanted friends to see them in his own handwriting before they were sterilized by the type-setter. "*That* was the poem, not the printed imitation," observed William Gass of Rilke's handwritten versions. "Writing by hand, mouthing by mouth: in each case you get a very strong physical sense of the emergence of language . . . print obliterates it; type has no drawl."

Renegades such as William Carlos Williams, T. S. Eliot, and John Ashbery did compose verse on a typewriter. Ashbery began typing poems when he found himself forgetting the ends of lines before his hand could transcribe them. In time he grew preternaturally attached to his circa 1930 Royal. Many writers have similar feelings for their typewriter, especially old manuals. Unlike a wimpy electric typewriter, one journalist pointed out, his Royal upright could take a punch thrown in creative anger and survive being drenched by frustrated teardrops or spilled whiskey. "I love the machine," said essayist Nick Lyons of his Underwood. "I love the sound it makes, the precise speed at which the keys move, a speed to which I've become accustomed; I like its responsiveness to my touch, even the pain it breeds in my shoulder when I've typed for too many hours, which tells me something. I like to correct my words by hand and even to retype a page, whereby I sometimes find more to correct. I like to feel the sensation of typing; I like to know, acutely, that I've put physical work into what I've written."

Andy Rooney spent most of his career as a journalist writing on an Underwood No. 5. When he tried using a computer, Rooney found that he wrote faster, but less accurately, and produced longer sentences. Many writers are horrified by word processors. They find the very idea of "processed words" appalling, the literary equivalent of Velveeta cheese. Such writers not only think that computer-aided writing is technology's triumph over art but worry that computers will add a layer of technophobia to their already fragile psyches.

My experience has been just the opposite. For the past decade, I've found my computer to be a major stress reducer. Not for composing. Like many writers, I draft by hand. But early on, my rough draft is thrown onto a computer screen. After that—even though I continue to take notes and revise by hand—the computer is where my writing gets done. This reduces both psychic and physical tension because changes are so easily made on the screen and mistakes so easily corrected. My computer corrects the most egregious spelling mistakes without so much as an arched eyebrow. It never gives me a funny look if I move material around in my text even one hundred times. This encourages me to be more flexible, to consider more alternatives. I can audition the same passage in five different chapters to see who wins the job. My computer also allows me to delete but save material in case I want to restore it. Such deletions nearly always improve a manuscript. I seldom restore any. But knowing I can is a comfort.

In general, computers give writing an elastic quality, which authors like myself find reassuring. My own worst writing fears have to do with indelibility. As long as I feel that mistakes can be corrected, improvements made, material added, such fears are tempered. The sense of *tentativeness* that computers lend to writing also makes the mailing of manuscripts less alarming. Heck, I tell myself, I can throw that sucker up on the screen and work it over one more time. Rather than submitting a completed manuscript (as if there were such a thing), I have a feeling of sending my publisher a tidy but tentative draft on a "What do you think?" basis.

Computer-aided writing allows one to dispense with

petty anxieties (will I have to type this page over?) and pay attention to what really matters: getting the words right. True, it can add technophobia to one's stew of fears, particularly after parts of manuscripts vanish in the computer's maw. But I like the exchange rate. On balance, I've found word processing has subtracted far more anxiety from the writing process than it's added. My computer has proved to be a first-rate fear buster: helpful, flexible, reassuring. It's my favorite totem.

Draft Dodgers

Once totems are in place, rituals completed, the gods appeased, one is faced with the task of actually writing. To some extent, there ain't nothin' to it but to do it. The page must be confronted. Nonetheless, writers do learn ways to avoid striding right up the ladder and onto the high wire.

"I linger over breakfast," said Kingsley Amis of his typical workday, "reading the papers, telling myself hypocritically that I've got to keep up with what's going on, but really staving off that dreadful time when I have to go to the typewriter."

James Jones found that it took him an hour and a half of "fiddling around" before he could work up the nerve to start writing. "I smoke half a pack of cigarettes," he said, "drink six or seven cups of coffee, read over what I wrote the day before. Finally there's no further excuse. I go to the typewriter."

When an interviewer told Edna O'Brien that Philip Roth said he spent several hours a day writing, every day of the year, the Irish novelist said she wrote for only a few hours in the morning, if that. "Did I tell you that I spend a lot of time moping?" she added. "Did Philip Roth say that he moped?"

Most writers do. Putzing around is their most popular getting-started technique; or else engaging in what novelist Robert Inman called "quality staring-out-the-window time." Sometimes there is naught to do but wait. Procrastination may reflect sloth and cowardice, but it can also be a true sign that one isn't ready to write. "When your Daemon is in charge," said Kipling, "do not try to think consciously. Drift, wait and obey." Writers like to dignify this process by calling it "waiting for the muse." But it's often difficult to distinguish muse waiting from simply fiddling around.

Many writers engage in anxiety-postponing exercises much as others do calisthenics. They listen to the radio, straighten their desk, catch up on correspondence. I'm always ambivalent about getting mail from colleagues. On the one hand, I'm usually happy to hear from a fellow writer. At the same time, I wonder why they're writing letters instead of manuscripts. E. B. White wrote so many letters that he often had no time left to write anything else. "Delay is natural to a writer," said White. "I walk around, straightening pictures on the wall, rugs on the floor—as though not until everything in the world was lined up and perfectly true could anybody reasonably expect me to set a word down on paper."

Before he actually began to write, White sometimes mixed himself a martini. "Just one," he said, "to give me the courage to get started." Such getting-started tactics are based on a respect for fear, an attempt to head it off, negotiate with the demon before it's transformed into full-scale panic. Some writers go straight from bed to their desk every morning before anxiety has a chance to grab them by the throat. Others read a little first. Annie Dillard scanned the index of first lines in poetry anthologies, hoping associations would get her brain clicking. Willa Cather read Bible passages before starting to write, seeking literary more than theological inspiration. Other writers won't read anything—not even a newspaper—for fear of interfering with whatever might be trying to worm its way up from their unconscious.

The most daunting time, of course, is when one actually puts pen to paper or fingers on a keyboard. That's when writers discover whether words will be forthcoming that day. Working writers learn to go easy on themselves at this point. They also discover ingenious methods of self-manipulation. The poet Hilda Doolittle began writing sessions by splashing ink on her clothes to give herself a feeling of freedom and indifference. Novelist Joseph McElroy said he found that using paper and pens stolen from the university where he taught, stationery stores, real estate agencies, banks, friends, and his daughter Hanna gave his imagination "a more disembodied feeling." A friend of Annie Dillard's ran errands to distract himself, then dashed home. Without even taking off his coat he went straight to his typewriter and started pushing keys in hopes of building momentum before he noticed what he was doing and seized up.

"Find tricks to keep yourself going," William Least Heat Moon once advised a group of aspiring writers. "Anything you can do to trick yourself out of panicking, do it." Moon told this group that in the early stages of a project, he used the cheapest paper and pencils he could find to symbolically diminish the gravity of his task. "What's he doing there?"

Moon said they might ask. "One thing he's doing is trying to trick his mind into not panicking at the sight of the blank paper: 'I'm not really writing. Just fooling around.' " Later, these early scratchings proved invaluable, said the author of *Blue Highways*. Having a scratch draft to work from gave him confidence.

Compose First, Worry Later

Before he even reviewed notes for an article, Calvin Trillin wrote a predraft—what he called "vomit-out"—of anything that came to mind. Sometimes Trillin wouldn't even look at the vomit-out, and he was terrified by the thought that anyone else might see it. Trillin found this document so embarrassing that he tore it up as soon as possible. Its composition was less a search for usable material than simply a way to kick-start his literary engine.

Like Trillin, working writers typically give themselves a lot of latitude in generating a first draft. Frank O'Connor said he composed short stories by writing "any sort of rubbish" until an outline began to emerge. Using a similar tactic, Christopher Isherwood tried to trick a good topic into rising from his unconscious by irritating it, "deliberately writing nonsense until it intervenes, as it were, saying, 'All right, you idiot, let me fix this.' " Raymond Chandler took this tactic one step farther. To start a new novel, Chandler first babbled into a tape recorder, then had a secretary transcribe his babbling for him to use as a rough draft.

Gail Godwin suggested approaching a difficult piece of writing as if it were a letter, telling your "correspondent" what you intended to write that day. That's how Isabel

Allende wrote novels: composing them as letters to her mother. Tom Wolfe used a similar tactic to do a spectacular end run on crippling writer's block early in his career. Wolfe had gone to Los Angeles to report for *Esquire* on car customizing. He then found himself unable to compose a coherent article from his notes. During an all-night, deadline-driven writing stint Wolfe finally typed up forty-nine pages of those notes as a memo to *Esquire*'s managing editor. The next day this editor called Wolfe to say that they were going to publish his memo untouched. It ran as "The Kandy-Kolored Tangerine-Flake Streamline Baby." The manic voice that Wolfe discovered this way has since reappeared in his many epoch-defining articles and books. With the proceeds from these books, Wolfe developed a taste for hand-tailored suits. That had two distinct benefits. For one thing, the fittings such suits required provided a welcome respite from writing. At the same time, Wolfe *had* to write in order to pay for the suits.

Reading about such writing tactics has made me realize how many I've unconsciously developed over the years. One key anxiety reducer I've learned is not to worry about beginnings. It's too easy to panic while waiting for the perfect opening. Fiction writers typically know the conclusion of a story they set out to write, but rarely know how it will begin. Good leads usually show up late. In my own writing and that of students, I generally find the best opening deep within a narrative. This opening only makes itself known as I read drafts, see what catches my eye, something that sets a tone, that gets the piece up and running. Knowing this, I don't concern myself with beginnings until the end. "The last thing one discovers in composing a work," said Blaise Pascal, "is what to put first."

Overall, I don't worry about order, form, or "getting it right" at the outset. I try to observe Ned Rorem's maxim: "Compose first, worry later." To me, this means taking some notes, doing a sketchy outline, then leaping right into the page's icy whiteness. Many of my colleagues won't write anything until they know exactly what they want to say. I *discover* what I want to say in the act of writing. This makes it necessary to throw away lots of premature work. My early drafts tend less to be publishable material than simply a way of taking the edge off anxiety, of making myself feel as though I'm "making progress." You thought there wasn't a book here? Ha! Just look at that stack of paper on my desk. No book indeed!

This approach resembles what we now call "free writing." A century ago it was called "automaticity." Every few years, a new oracle breaks through to propose some form of free writing as the best way to conquer writing anxiety. Just write spontaneously, the advice usually goes, before your conscious mind has a chance to remind the unconscious one of how much peril you're in. Forget form, structure, grammar, spelling, outlining, and even writing well. *Just write.* Within reason, this is good advice. Free writing can loosen the hand, tickle the muse, and soothe writing nerves. By writing freely, you're essentially saying, I'll ignore my anxiety about getting it right and write anyway, on a provisional basis. One novelist learned to circumvent her fear by telling herself at the beginning of each writing session that she was just going to jot some things down so she could change them later. In a variation on this technique, writing coach Brenda Ueland told students who were paralyzed by the fear of writing badly to do just that: write as bad a story as they could possibly write. This assignment gave them "the courage to venture a few little sentences," reported Ueland. "And since everybody who is human cannot say a sentence without revealing something—something mild or violent or waggish in their souls—or without having something fine in it, I would point this out. Courage would expand and they would gradually write more."

Such tactics are good tactics, as far as they go. They just don't go far enough. Any writer who aspires to publish on a regular basis must learn to follow through. The product of free writing is like a sculptor's wet clay. It gives the writer essential materials to work with and a dose of confidence. But learning how to fashion a statue from clay or a manuscript from free writing is the real test of nerve. At this point a workmanlike approach is called for.

Over time, productive writers develop work habits that would make an accountant gasp with admiration. After wasting too many years waiting for genius to strike, Stendhal finally settled on a regimen of "twenty lines a day, genius or not." Like Stendhal, many writers—including Norman Mailer, Ernest Hemingway, and Graham Greene—assigned themselves production quotas to meet as if they were Soviet workers fulfilling five-year plans. Arthur Hailey wrote his daily quota—six hundred words—at the top of a pad, then wouldn't allow himself to put the pad down until he'd fulfilled it. Anthony Trollope assigned himself not only a quota of words but a time limit in which to produce them. With his watch ticking away before him, the British novelist routinely wrote 250 words every quarter hour. Trollope also kept a diary of his daily output to ensure that he made steady progress, "so that if at any time I have slipped into idleness for a day or two, the record of that idleness has been there, staring me in the face." By this means, Trollope produced more than seventy books while employed full-time at the post office.

The quota approach to writing sounds compulsive: the writer as word counter. But quotas serve an important psychic function. They keep writers working despite the normal, almost irresistible urge to quit. Writers need some gimmick—often many gimmicks—to keep themselves going despite their anxiety. Rituals are one. Free writing is another. Word quotas are a third. But don't gimmicks produce drivel? Sometimes. Even drivel can be fixed, however. And in its midst one sometimes finds gold. When starting a new book, Philip Roth often wrote a hundred pages or more before one paragraph turned up that was alive. Going over his first six months' work, Roth would underline a sentence here, a phrase there that had some life, then type these onto a single page. That's right: *one page* to show for six months of literary engine revving. William Maxwell used a similar tactic. He looked for good sentences in bad paragraphs, then cut these sentences out and glued them to a piece of paper.

Paper selection feels psychologically important to some writers. Like Least Heat Moon, Conrad Aiken used cheap yellow paper for early drafts because he thought it looked less "responsible." Joan Didion developed a multicolored system: yellow paper for note taking, pale blue for putting notes into shape, and good white bond when the end was near, when it seemed that only by making the commitment to use expensive paper with a watermark could she possibly complete her manuscript.

Block Busting

Using different colors of paper is one among many tactics Michael Crichton has tried to jerk himself out of writing ruts. On one occasion Crichton locked himself in a Boston motel to complete a book, then found himself so bored that he wrote vigorously in order to win his release. He's also attempted to shake off writing lethargy by consulting psychics, soaking in isolation tanks, climbing mountains, and swimming among sharks off Tahiti. "Adversity isn't bad," said Crichton of such block-busting techniques, "because it gives you something specific to be frustrated about: writing when it's too hot, too cold, too close to a deadline, or on a typewriter that doesn't work right. Sneaking up on it sometimes helps: I've found I can be very productive for an hour before dinner, because there obviously isn't enough time to really do anything, so I can tell myself I'm just screwing around."

There are as many approaches to busting blocks as there are writers who employ them. T. S. Eliot battled writer's block by writing poems in French, Joseph Conrad by playing chess with his son, Irving Stone by weeding his garden. Kurt Vonnegut found swimming or any other form of "disorienting" exercise a big help. John Cheever took regular breaks to swim, ice-skate, or roam the aisles of discount stores in search of inspiration. Shifting back and forth between writing by hand and typing helped Norman Mailer get beyond arid periods while writing *Barbary Shore*.

"If you are in difficulties with a book," suggested H. G. Wells, "try the element of surprise: attack it at an hour when it isn't expecting it." This was one way Gail Godwin learned to outfox her "watcher" (the inner critic who kept an eye on her as she worked): looking for times to write when she was off guard. Other tactics Godwin found helpful included writing too fast and in unexpected places and times; working when tired; writing in purple ink on the back of charge card statements; and jotting down whatever came to mind while a tea kettle boiled, using its whistle as a deadline. "Deadlines are a great way to outdistance the watcher," advised Godwin.

Many writers can't get serious until a due date looms before them like a ticking bomb. E. B. White produced a remarkable body of work under the pressure of weekly and monthly deadlines. But when he took a year off to produce something "significant," White produced virtually nothing and cut the year short. Deadline-driven writers like him learn to sign contracts with delivery dates in the not too distant future. Some create artificial deadlines by announcing them to friends or by promising partial drafts to their publisher. Other writers find deadlines paralyzing. Katherine Anne Porter was one. Porter said of her reaction when publishers asked for work at the time she'd agreed to deliver it: "Pressure of that sort simply throws me into a catatonic state, paralyzes my will, muddles my mind, and hurts my feelings." If they can afford it, deadline-phobic writers do better not to sign contracts in advance. Any number of writers will offer only finished work to a publisher.

For most writers—deadline driven or not—anxiety peaks as the time to evict their literary offspring draws near. Doing so is never easy. The annals of publishing are littered with promised manuscripts that were still in their writers' hands years after the due date. Since no piece of writing ever feels complete, authors find ways to work up the nerve to let go of it anyway.

Within reason, mailing a manuscript because you're sick of it is as good a reason as any. Bernard Malamud said he knew a novel was finished when he could no longer stand working on it. The inner voice telling us it's had enough of a project can be wise. But that voice is not always reliable. I've known too many writers who mailed early drafts of work because they were tired of working on them. Their products read like it: half-baked. Alternatively, one risks becoming a Ralph Ellison or Henry Roth, spending decades fiddling with novels-in-progress. Either approach is a poor response to jitters. Most writers learn to strike a balance between getting rid of something too soon or too late. John dos Passos said the time to finish a manuscript was when revisions were making it worse rather than better. The only problem is knowing when that time is. I find that once I start changing revised material back to its original form, it's time to think about writing "The End" and look about for a mailing envelope.

Writers' Hours

Alberto Moravia was once so miserably in love that he wandered the streets of Rome hoping a car would run him over. "That was in the afternoon, of course," said Moravia. "In the morning I work."

Like Moravia, most writers work in the morning. Anthony Trollope thought the key to productivity was being at his desk by 5:30 every morning. Paul Valéry started writing at 5:00 A.M. and seldom wrote past 9:00. Faulkner considered his writing day over by 10:30 or 11:00. For most writers, the morning is a fertile time. Sleep has cleared their minds and left a clear path for the unconscious to stride onto the page. Concentration is easier before the day's errands, phone calls, and news from the Middle East have cluttered their heads. The contrast in quality between morning and postmorning writing can be so great that many writers don't even try to write after lunch. Early on, Gabriel García Márquez felt guilty about working only in the morning and made himself write in the afternoons too. But after finding that he invariably had to redo his afternoon work, Márquez gave it up. That's been my own experience. Since most of my postlunch writing has to be rewritten anyway, I seldom do any. From 9:00 A.M. to 1:00 P.M. I can write as though in a trance. Trying to produce anything in the afternoon makes me feel like an ox pulling a loaded cart with sticky wheels. At night I might as well be writing in Swahili.

Not all writers are morning writers. Anthony Burgess sometimes did his most inspired work in the afternoon. Jean Auel and Bette Bao Lord wrote their novels late at night. As a young woman, Margaret Atwood did too, while studying and teaching during the day. When her afternoons freed up, Atwood became a postlunch writer. But when she was finally free to write whenever she chose, that also proved problematic. "I used to spend the morning procrastinating and worrying," Atwood said, "then plunge into the manuscript in a frenzy of anxiety around 3:00 when it looked as though I might not get anything done. Since the birth of my daughter, I've had to cut down on the procrastination. I still try to spend the afternoons writing, though the preliminary period of anxiety is somewhat shorter. I suppose this is a more efficient use of time."

What do schedules have to do with courage and fear? More than is apparent. One key to reducing anxiety and increasing resolve is learning how to exploit personal peak periods. Writing is not only easier then but also less alarming. Tasks that feel like climbing Mt. Everest when you're not alert can feel like a stroll around Walden Pond when you are. No one doubts that body clocks influence productivity. Their impact on bravery is less appreciated. Identifying the time of day when you feel bravest and trying to write then is an essential aspect of fear management. For some, that's in the afternoon or at night. But most of us are more confident at dawn than at dusk. "In the night I am constantly haunted by what I am trying to realize," said Monet. "I rise broken with fatigue each morning. But the coming of the dawn gives me courage."

Customized Fear Management

A wise writer I knew modulated his fears by writing at several levels: (1) for publication by publishers; (2) for publication by himself; (3) for friends only; (4) for his trunk. By not confusing the four, he was able to happily write at each level.

All working writers devise their own program for keeping fear at bay. Although writing nerves never vanish, they do become more manageable over time. No magic strategy exists that will turn an anxious novice into a self-assured veteran. Since courage points vary so much from writer to writer, there is no one-size-fits-all program to recommend. Developing writing courage involves learning about one's working style and how it's best manipulated.

Some writers keep a notebook. They find that jotting down random ideas, observations, and snatches of conversation provides invaluable grist for their writing mill. Part of the thinking here is that an idea not recorded at the moment of inspiration may be lost forever. Their notebook gives them comfort. For that very reason, William Maxwell found he wrote better if he *didn't* jot things down as they occurred to him. "I like the insecurity and the danger of not keeping a notebook," he explained.

When I'd just started writing, a novelist advised me in strictest terms *never* to discuss what I was working on for fear of dissipating its energy. This turned out to be nearly an article of faith among fiction writers. But there are heretics. Though cognizant of the danger, Toni Morrison admitted that she sometimes found it helpful to discuss work-in-progress with colleagues. Aldous Huxley had no problem at all telling others what he was writing. Sometimes he even welcomed the opportunity, thinking that describing what he was working on might give him a clearer sense of what he was trying to accomplish.

That's been my experience. After a year or so of religiously taking my friend's advice, I drank too much at a party one night and let a few words slip out about what I was working on. To my surprise, those with whom I was talking had some helpful reactions. In the back-and-forth that followed, my own thinking was stimulated, sharpened. Since then I've made a point of talking with others about what I'm writing. Doing so has rewarded me with ideas, leads, people to interview. Sometimes I find myself phrasing an idea better in person than I have on paper. Then I jot down the better words (always carrying pen and paper for that purpose) to weave into my manuscript. For many writers, discussing work-in-progress raises their level of anxiety; for me, it quells my fears.

This leads to the question, Why don't more writers seek counsel? Discussing work with colleagues and showing them manuscripts seems like a sensible strategy—and is for many writers. But not for all.

8

A Little Help from Friends

Solitude, competitiveness and grief
are the unavoidable lot of a writer
only when there is no organization
or network to which he can turn.
—*Toni Morrison*

John Ciardi once dismissed poetry workshops as "hired
sympathy." Yet "hired sympathy" was exactly what Maxine
Kumin said she was looking for in a poetry course she took
at the Boston Center for Adult Education in 1957. This
class was taught by the poet John Holmes. Another member was Anne Sexton. Since Sexton had been too scared to
call the Boston Center, a friend called for her. Taking
Holmes's course proved to be a turning point in Anne
Sexton's literary aspirations. "The most important aspect of
that class," she later recalled, "was that I felt I belonged
somewhere."

After meeting at the Boston Center, Sexton and Kumin
became fast friends. The two fledgling poets had special
telephone lines installed in their homes so they could spend
hours each day going over poems. "I call Maxine every

other line," Sexton once said. Kumin recalled that their conversations focused on such practical questions as whether an image worked; where a poem ended; what was the right beginning; whether a given rhyme was best. On a deeper level, Kumin found that this working friendship gave her needed encouragement and a touch of the Sexton wildness her own poetry lacked.

Sexton herself became a great course taker and conference attender. When the Boston Center class ended, she went to the Antioch Writer's Conference in Ohio. Sexton then joined Kumin and others in an informal poetry workshop led by John Holmes that met twice a month in members' homes. Participants critiqued each others' poems and helped prepare them for publication. Sometimes they did so rather loudly. Whenever Kumin's three children saw her setting out cups and glasses for a workshop meeting, they would ask suspiciously, "Who's coming?" After being told, her kids would groan, "The poets! Oh, no! Now we'll never get any sleep. Can we go sleep in the room over the garage?"

For Kumin, the workshop's raucous meetings were "almost violently productive." They were for Sexton too. According to biographer Diane Wood Middlebrook, Anne Sexton found that "the unbridled excitement of the group process led frequently to inspired revision." Within its first year, four of the workshop's five regular members—including Sexton and Kumin—had published books of poetry. (Both women, of course, went on to win Pulitzer prizes.) Middlebrook thought the group's critiquing contributed to the high quality of finish each book displayed. This experience convinced Kumin of the value of workshops, "at least of good workshops where passion and empathy mingle and a poet can try out a new poem on trained and thoughtful ears."

Based on the experience of Maxine Kumin, Anne Sexton, and so many others, it would seem self-evident that writers can benefit from the help of advance readers. To some writers, that's not self-evident at all.

To Show or Not to Show

Vladimir Nabokov thought circulating early drafts of one's work was like passing around samples of sputum.

Jonathan Swift read works-in-progress to his servants, assuming that if they could make sense of it, anyone could.

Ishmael Reed gave public readings of fiction he was writing, revising as he read.

Philip Larkin never showed drafts of his poems to anyone. "What would be the point?" he asked.

To show or not to show? Writers are all over the board on this question. For some, circulating work-in-progress soothes their nerves; for others, it's like massaging them with sandpaper. Fay Weldon's only immutable writing rule was not to show anything incomplete to anyone. Anne Tyler, Mario Puzo, and Joyce Carol Oates sent manuscripts only to their publisher. "I wouldn't show a novel to anyone who couldn't write me a check," said mystery writer Sharyn McCrumb. Others show and suffer. Nadine Gordimer sometimes sent manuscripts to colleagues for comment, then found herself "sick with apprehension" while they were reading them.

Among those who do show work, there is much variety in whom they consider qualified to see it. Novelist Russell Hoban shared unfinished work *only* with his psychiatrist.

William Maxwell changed the ending of *The Folded Leaf* at the behest of his analyst, Theodor Reik. When unsure about the plot of *Pleading Guilty*, Scott Turow sent copies of his novel-in-progress to eight nonliterary professionals for a reading. More often, writers seek the counsel of peers. Before they became close friends, Saul Bellow sent John Berryman a nearly completed manuscript of *The Adventures of Augie March* to review. Later, Bellow and his neighbor Richard Stern got together regularly to read each other's work-in-progress; "trying things out," as Stern put it.

Some writers feel most comfortable showing work to family members. Isabel Allende gave manuscripts to her mother to read, Marianne Moore to her brother, Jim Harrison to his oldest daughter. Robert Stone said his wife was the only "civilian" he'd consult when stuck on a novel. Scott Turow thought the fact that his wife was an exhibiting painter helped her be a critical but compassionate first reader of his work. Presumably spouses get consulted so often because they can be candid. But that's not always the case. "He certainly didn't ever want me to say I didn't like something," admitted John Steinbeck's widow, Elaine. "He wanted me to say, 'That's wonderful,' and I did."

In the guise of "seeking feedback," many writers are trolling for compliments. When they ask for your opinion of their work, too often they mean your praise. "It's my experience that very few writers, young or old, are really seeking advice when they give out their work to be read," said John Irving. "They want support; they want someone to say 'Good job.' "

That's why it's so hard to get candor from advance readers. They're never clear about how much honesty is expected of them. Courage is necessary not only to write but to critique. Any advance critic with a gram of sensitivity senses how vulnerable writers are, especially those who have just wrestled a bucking manuscript to the ground. If involved with the writer personally, a manuscript reader will be reluctant to hurt that person's feelings or put their friendship to the test. More than one friendship has been jeopardized by an overly candid response. After eating lunch with Benjamin Jowett, master of Oxford's Balliol College, Alfred Tennyson read him a newly written poem. "I shouldn't publish that if I were you," commented Jowett. Replied Tennyson, "If it comes to that, Master, the sherry you gave us at lunch was downright filthy."

As an aspiring writer, William Faulkner was friendly with Sherwood Anderson. Anderson sometimes read stories written by his young colleague. He was impressed by Faulkner's talent, though wary of his facility with words. The older writer may also have been a bit threatened by the younger one. When Faulkner told Anderson that he'd begun a novel, Anderson said, "My God" and stalked out of his friend's apartment. After Faulkner completed that novel (*Soldier's Pay*), he met Anderson's wife on the street. She asked him how his book was going. He told her it was finished. Mrs. Anderson said her husband was worried about that. "Sherwood says that he will make a trade with you," she continued. "If he doesn't have to read your manuscript he will tell his publisher to accept it."

"Done," replied Faulkner.

I once read a dog-eared manuscript for a friend of mine in Philadelphia. My friend had published one novel but couldn't get this one into print. He asked if I'd look at it. Reluctantly, I agreed. It was obvious why no one wanted to publish this novel. The book was lifeless: indifferently written and badly researched. Following what scant praise I could muster, I pointed out that there were no Dutch-style windmills in Pennsylvania Dutch country as he'd written (*Dutch* being derivative of *Deutsch*, for the German-Americans who lived there). I wondered if taking a drive through that area might not only be pleasant but give him firsthand material with which to freshen his prose. My friend didn't appreciate this response. In fact, he told me, realizing how little regard I had for his writing made him question our very friendship. It was never the same thereafter.

Obviously, the question of whether to circulate work-in-progress, and if so to whom, has many dimensions. In theory, authors should be able to step outside their work and field comments about it with the cold eye of a stockbroker reviewing investments. No writer could be that detached, however. One whose work has been found wanting is about as objective as a parent whose child has been criticized. The admonition not to take criticism "personally" is nearly impossible for writers to abide. If they've put themselves on the page—as they should—how can they take responses to their writing any other way?

That's one reason even successful writers sometimes respond as if touched with a red-hot poker at the merest hint of a rebuke. When Robert Benchley's daughter-in-law told John O'Hara that she liked *Pal Joey* even better the second time she saw it, O'Hara asked, "What was wrong with it the first time?" In the midst of favorably reviewing a book by H. G. Wells, Leonard Woolf cited someone *else's* negative assessment of his friend's work. After reading Woolf's review, Wells drafted a letter of retraction for him to sign and publish. (Woolf refused.)

There's no mystery about why writers so often respond to any whisper of criticism with a spirited self-defense. It's not their writing that they feel is being picked at; it's their souls. This understandable attitude can be a serious obstacle to improving one's writing. A self-defensive reaction to a critique of one's work may or may not be justified but is nearly always beside the point. Once that writing is published, readers will probably have similar responses. But writers can't be at readers' sides to defend themselves.

Some writers try to finesse this dilemma by circulating unpublished work only after securing assurances that a reader won't say anything "discouraging." Such an approach is shortsighted and unfair to the manuscript reader. There are better ways to seek reassurance than imposing on the goodwill of others. We all crave praise and loathe criticism. If psychologically cunning—as most writers are—we convey our need for encouragement. But all we're really doing by pleading for reassurance in the guise of comment is putting off the day of reckoning; postponing what we'll eventually hear from editors, reviewers, and readers. The most useful response to a manuscript pulls no punches. If an advance reader has found flaws in our work that need fixing, better we should hear about them while there's still time to do so. Or—if we just can't bear the idea of having our work criticized—spare advance readers and ourselves the frustration by not circulating work-in-progress.

Rather than try to manipulate responses, writers who feel the need for a manuscript critique should choose readers carefully, then try to hear what they have to say. It would be inhuman not to feel defensive about anything less than raves. But there are ways to field mixed advance reviews without looking about for a razor blade with which to slit one's wrists.

One way is to be systematic. After writing several drafts of a novel, Jeffrey Archer sent copies to six readers for review. He then gave a revised version to six other readers. Based on their response, Archer completed a final draft for one last jury of half a dozen new readers. "I know a lot of writers won't listen to criticism from anyone about their writing, they just finish it and that's it," he explained. "That isn't my way."

Henry Adams had his manuscripts set in type and bound. Adams then circulated these prepublication books among friends, inviting them to write reactions in extra-wide margins. In a similar spirit, essayist Phillip Lopate came to regard the circulation of photocopied manuscripts as a form of advance publication that in some ways was more satisfying than the actual kind. "When I finish something I can't wait," he explained. "I've been lonely with it so I publish it in *samizdat*. It's as though the piece has been published when someone who's capable of understanding it receives it. That's the true publication."

My own approach is to show all or parts of work-in-progress to selected readers. I do this because I'd much rather hear about problems in my writing from them than from book buyers who feel they've wasted money on my published book. Getting critiques from several people whom I trust also helps me put the subsequent response of my editor in perspective. This way, the editor becomes a member of the jury rather than a single judge. From past, painful experience, however, I've learned to show advance readers only nearly completed manuscripts. Before learning this lesson, I sometimes made the mistake of circulating drafts at too early a stage. The reactions I got from rough-draft readers were usually ones of horror. "This is a mess!" They were right. The work's pattern was visible only to its author.

In the precomputer era, I took a small suitcase with cut-and-pasted chapters to my editor in New York. This valise was presented to him at the end of a long day. We had agreed to discuss it over dinner that night. My editor sighed, rubbed his red-veined eyes, then trudged off holding my suitcase like a sack of dumbbells. At dinner we talked about my "manuscript." Undoubtedly the editor was more horrified than he let on by its chaotic state. He did ask if I'd ever thought about buying a word processor.

Such anxiety-raising experiences taught me to never circulate material that isn't a revision or two away from completion. The only person to whom I'll show something less complete is my wife, Muriel (who's learned over the years not to be too unnerved by disorderly drafts, or at least not to say so if she is).

When choosing readers to review manuscripts, I try to keep clear goals in mind. The most important criterion is that such readers be like those I hope will read my book. I've generally gotten the most help from those chosen less for their literary credentials than for their judgment and willingness to speak up. The best advance readers of all are those able to articulate the reactions of a prototypical reader (e.g.: "This point isn't clear," "That part's slow," "This got my interest," "That's a cliché"). I pay careful attention to every point made. This doesn't mean giving them all equal weight or incorporating every change suggested. I do try to stay open, and respond to comments that ring a bell with me; ones that confirm a weakness I'm concerned about or perhaps encourage me to retain material I'd thought about deleting.

When enough eyes examine a manuscript, patterns of response are usually more helpful than individual ones. Ten readers reviewed a manuscript of this book. The group ranged from much-published to aspiring writers. So many of them had trouble with my original first chapter that I rewrote it entirely. Since most found the second half of the book stronger than the first, I spent extra time revising early sections. Many wanted to hear more from the author himself, and in the revised version, they do. Those who wanted more writing samples got them. My advance readers caught all manner of typographical errors, punctuation mistakes, and grammar goofs. Some reactions were common to most readers, but others were singular or even contradictory. Although many thought I quoted other writers too often, one colleague said, "I particularly enjoyed all the quotes."

Learning how to assess feedback is an acquired skill. All reactions are not equally helpful. Some can be stunningly wrongheaded. On the eve of *Stuart Little*'s publication, E. B. White got a letter from an eminent children's librarian who had read a galley of the book. She found it, as White recalled, "non-affirmative, inconclusive, [and] unfit for children." The librarian suggested he cancel *Stuart Little*'s publication. White thought the matter over and—to the gratitude of generations of readers—decided to stay the course. "I was shook up by the letter," he later said, "but not deflected."

Written critiques are easier to deal with than spoken ones. They can be reviewed and assessed in booklike privacy. Verbal responses are harder to hear over all the alarm bells they set off. Whenever an advance reader responds to a draft of my work in person or by phone, I take copious notes, as if interviewing that person. This note-taking: (1) makes me pay careful attention; (2) provides information I can review later in a less charged atmosphere; (3) forces me to stifle defensive reactions. That, in turn, encourages my reader-critic to respond in more candid and helpful detail.

Where Have You Gone, Maxwell Perkins?

While going over a manuscript with an editor, I take notes too; lots of notes. For the very same reasons: to force myself to *listen* and not respond defensively. The nearly irresistible impulse is to argue back. ("Can't you see that . . . ?") The general idea is that one's editor lacks the acuity to appreciate literary brilliance. Sometimes that's true. More often, an editor (one earning her pay, anyway) has seen things the writer missed because he was too protective of his offspring.

Doris Grumbach got detailed suggestions on every page of the manuscript of her novel *Chamber Music* from copy editor Faith Sale. On first reading, Sale's suggestions made Grumbach furious. She thought her novel was perfect as submitted. On reflection, Grumbach realized that Sale had spotted flaws in her work. This depressed her. Just as she was rereading the copy editor's notes and cursing, Grumbach's overall editor—Henry Robbins—called to say he figured she'd be feeling low right about then, but to keep in mind that Sale's comments were not about anything crucial and shouldn't disturb her. Grumbach considered Robbins's timely call "a miraculous kind of sympathy." After his death she asked Faith Sale to be her editor.

Like brie, editorial feedback is most palatable when it's aged. That's why letters from editors are best glanced over, then set aside to mellow. A few days' respite, a stiff drink, and reminders from your loved ones that they still love you work wonders. Looking over correspondence and conversation notes from that perspective, I often find much of value. Before Frank Rich became a two-fisted drama critic and columnist for the *New York Times*, he was a magazine editor who rejected an assigned piece of mine with two pages of reasons. This was quite unusual. Editors seldom explain themselves in such detail. Once I got over my hurt feelings and reread Rich's letter, I saw much to be said for his comments. Eventually, another magazine bought the piece, revised in light of Rich's critique.

Critiquing a writer's work is an art form. Even the best editors find that process challenging. No matter how experienced writers are, going over their manuscript with an editor is an anxious affair. Editors know this and learn how to lay it on with a tablespoon, if not a trowel. T. S. Eliot said that editors should always tell authors that their writing was better than it actually was; not a lot better but a little. Some writers don't care what an editor says. They deal with editorial feedback by ignoring it. Erle Stanley Gardner once attached a note to a manuscript he sent to a magazine that advised, "It's a damn good story. If you have any comments, write them on the back of a check."

There are two basic reasons writers spurn editorial suggestions. Some are so sure of their writing that suggestions feel superfluous. "The good artist believes that nobody is good enough to give him advice," said Faulkner. "He has supreme vanity." Others are so *un*sure of their writing that they don't dare listen to comments about it. Unfortunately, the latter often passes for the former, among young writers especially. Early in his career, Richard Yates spurned suggestions from editors. He thought his writing didn't need any. As he grew older, however, the novelist yearned for more editorial help than he got. "I no longer feel . . . that everything I do in final draft is perfect," Yates now admitted.

In theory, editors can not only improve manuscripts but buck up anxious writers and calm their tattered nerves. Some can. In the acknowledgments to a compilation of her radio interviews, Susan Stamberg credited editor Joni Evans with "anxiety-ridding guidance." Any number of writers have dedicated books to their editors. Thomas Wolfe's dedication of *Of Time and the River* to Maxwell Perkins described him as "a great editor and a brave and honest man, who stuck to the writer of this book through times of bitter hopelessness and doubt and would not let him give in to his own despair."

Editors aren't the only ones who can throw a rope to writers drowning in a sea of anxiety. When touring to promote a book, authors discover that their publicist's reassuring voice is the first one they hear in the morning and the last at night. Despite the obligatory bellyaching, authors tend to enjoy the lionizing of a publicity tour. Robert MacNeil once bumped into Saul Bellow as he was about to start promoting his latest novel. MacNeil observed that books written by Nobel laureates might be thought to sell themselves. Why did he subject himself to the ordeal of touring? "Writing is a very lonely business," replied Bellow. "You get cabin fever. You want to get out and meet people."

I was once on an author's panel with Joyce Carol Oates, who introduced her remarks by saying, "The reason we all look so happy up here is because we're not at home

writing." On another occasion I heard Oates repeat this
observation, adding, "When writers are out in public the
laughter level is high, and they're very buoyant—even
without alcohol because they're not at home feeling like
they're taking a test." This leads to the question, Why
don't writers get out and about more? Some do. Henry
James, Paul Claudel, and Paul Valéry were great boulevar-
diers. "I like living too much to be seated all day at a
desk," said Pablo Neruda. "I like to put myself in the
goings-on of life, of my house, of politics, and of nature. I
am forever coming and going." Other writers are appalled
by the very idea of that much carrying on by an author.
Proust regarded an hour spent in the company of others as
an hour lost to writing forever. Erskine Caldwell said the
characters in his books were his only friends, and ought to
be. "You cannot be both a good socializer and a good
writer," said Caldwell. "You have to choose."

Courses, Conferences, and Groups

To open a lecture at Columbia University, Sinclair Lewis
asked the students, "How many of you here are really
serious about becoming writers?" Hands shot up all around
the room. "Well, why the hell aren't you all home writing?" roared Lewis.

This is far from an uncommon attitude. Course taking
and conference attending are regarded with deep suspicion
by many working writers. "How can you teach writing?"
they ask. Probably you can't. Writing *techniques* can be
taught. But that's only one purpose served by writing
classes and not necessarily the most important one. Their
more important lessons are conveyed in the realm of the

spirit. When an interviewer asked Anne Sexton what a writing class could offer students, Sexton replied, "Courage, of course. That's the most important ingredient."

Writing programs can provide a safe haven, a sparsely filled theater in which to practice lines before facing the trauma of an audience. The best thing writing courses can do is help participants develop the will to write. They provide a setting where aspiring writers can look inside their hearts and find the courage to tell us what they see. That lesson is infinitely more valuable than any about story structure, use of dialogue, or time-shifting techniques.

I've found this attitude toward course taking common among daring people ranging from rock climbers through entrepreneurs to stand-up comedians. Our stereotype of such adventurers is that they dive into deep water without hesitating. This hasn't been my experience. Other than some self-destructive hot dogs, few of the ones I've met were reckless risk takers. Most looked long and hard before they leaped. Sky divers took training classes and did tandem jumps before going solo. Entrepreneurs enrolled in courses on small business management. Aspiring comedians joined comedy workshops. Ostensibly such course taking was to learn skills. In fact—as most freely admitted—what a class really did was help them screw up their courage in a sheltered setting. "You can't risk failure in front of the camera," actress Jessica Walters explained of an acting class she took late in her career. "I can do things here I'd never get hired for."

Courses and groups serve a similar purpose for writers. An effective way to deal with writing anxiety—at the outset especially—is to take refuge in a class, conference, or ongoing group. The list of successful writers who have benefited from such gatherings is a long one. After her novels began to win acclaim, Gail Godwin tried unsuccessfully to locate and thank the teacher who taught her at the City Literary Institute in London. E. B. White got early encouragement from monthly meetings of Cornell's Manuscript Club.

Amy Tan attended the Squaw Valley Community of Writers when she was thirty-three, hoping to break out of the technical writing she'd been doing for years and spread her wings into fiction. The story she submitted was ripped apart by a conference teacher named Molly Giles. Afterward, Giles invited Tan to join a writers' group in San Francisco. Members of this group met weekly, often in Tan's house, sometimes eating cookies baked by the aspiring author herself. They read works-in-progress to one another. Tan found this method invaluable because she got a "real reader's response" to her work, on the spot. During three years of weekly meetings, Tan added, she learned to listen, and to *see* fiction. Several stories Tan read to the group were published. Out of them grew *The Joy Luck Club*. In her acknowledgments to that novel, Tan writes, "The author is grateful to her weekly writer's group for kindness and criticism during the writing of this book."

Like Amy Tan, Toni Morrison first got the idea that she could write fiction while taking part in a writers' group. This one met at Howard University, where Morrison had gone to teach when she was thirty. She joined the group mainly to meet people. Since members were expected to share work-in-progress, Morrison read some stories she'd written in high school. When these were gone, she was forced to write a new one. Morrison wrote and read her group a story about a black girl who wanted blue eyes. This story provided the basis for her first novel, *The Bluest Eye*.

I suspect more writers have been helped by writers' gatherings than will say so out loud. Such a disclosure lays them open to ridicule from colleagues who think that no *real* writer needs this type of crutch. Ezra Pound once invited Robert Frost to join a weekly meeting of poets who went over each others' work. "That sounds like a parlor game to me," needled Frost, "and I'm a serious artist." Pound laughed and never renewed the invitation.

Why are so many writers so reluctant to seek or accept each other's help? Some say it's a matter of principle. Among male writers especially, there's a lot of hubris about writers being Lone Rangers with a silver pen in their holster. Many consider themselves the last of the rugged individualists. Just as soldiers earn medals by braving gunfire, they seem to feel, writers prove their mettle by enduring solitude. "Writing, at its best, is a lonely life," said Hemingway when accepting his Nobel Prize for literature (in absentia). "Organizations for writers palliate the writer's loneliness, but I doubt if they improve his writing. He grows in public stature as he sheds his loneliness and after his work deteriorates. For he does his work alone and if he is a good enough writer he must face eternity, or the lack of it, each day."

Another reason writers of both sexes don't seek each other's company more is that they are shy. One motivation for becoming a writer is that one feels more comfortable dealing with written than spoken words. When she was interviewed for *Paris Review*, Cynthia Ozick *typed* her responses for the interviewer sitting before her. When he wasn't composing poems, Judson Jerome sat before his computer screen by the hour conducting electronic conversations with faceless colleagues around the country. Jerome told me that these conversations were the most comfortable ones he'd ever enjoyed; the closest to actual writing.

A final reason for the bad odor groups have among working writers is that too many are taken over by those who gather better than they write. Would-be writers often join them in lieu of writing. At best, they carry the same tattered, much-critiqued piece of writing from group to group as a ticket of admission. "Workshop junkies" is what poet Diane Wakoski has called those who can't leave the gentle embrace of sympathetic colleagues to seek their fortune among hard-eyed editors. For them, classes and groups become a way to play at being a "writer" without doing much serious writing.

These legitimate concerns make those who *do* write seriously wary of groups. But I don't think that they're the real reason writers won't offer each other more aid and comfort. The more basic reason is that writers are scared of each other. Scared they'll steal each other's ideas. Scared that colleagues won't like their work. Scared that if they accept one another's help, even their company, it will reflect poorly on their ability to make it on their own. And— worst of all—scared that other writers will do better and show them up. As John Updike's writer mother once told him about his success, "Frankly, Johnny, I'd rather it had been me."

One reason for writing is to create an alternative universe in which we play God. As monotheists, we see no room in that universe for another deity. Bennett Cerf once made the mistake of spontaneously inviting William Faulkner to join him and his houseguest, Sinclair Lewis, at Cerf's home after dinner. Lewis didn't like the idea. "This is *my* night," he told Random House's founder. "Haven't you been a publisher long enough to understand that I don't want to share it with some other author?" Cerf called Faulkner back to cancel the invitation. Lewis went to bed. Cerf and his wife stayed up in the living room two floors below. After a time they heard their guest shouting from upstairs, "Bennett! Bennett!" Lewis sounded agitated, so they rushed to the stairs to ask what had happened. "I just wanted to be sure you hadn't slipped out to see Faulkner," he explained.

P. G. Wodehouse claimed never to have envied a colleague. He realized nonetheless how difficult it was for writers to be friends. Wodehouse recalled the time when Somerset Maugham passed him on the street. "He looked at me and I looked at him, and we were thinking the same thing: 'Oh, my God, shall we have to stop and talk?' Fortunately, we didn't." When an interviewer observed that writers didn't seem to get along with each other very well, Wodehouse agreed. "I think they're jealous of each other," he said. "I do get along with them superficially, if everything's all right. But you feel they're resenting you, rather."

Be that as it may, this approach to colleagues is self-defeating. One of the best things about being a writer is that one's own victory needn't be at someone else's expense. Too often we approach writing as if it were a tennis match. I win; you lose. A more realistic, more positive model is that of an orchestra where the better each performer sounds, the better they all sound. Writing can be approached the same way. My victory needn't depend on your defeat. If you write better than me, I hope I'll feel pleased for you. I know I'll feel jealous, spiteful, competitive, and spurred to do better myself. In the process, perhaps we'll both improve and the general level of writing will rise.

Give Groups a Chance

There are times when encouragement from others is essential to keep a writer going. Groups may not be able to help members become better writers, directly, but they can be a source of company, support, and useful shoptalk. At the very least, their meetings provide respite from the isolation that makes up so much of any writer's day. They are a few hours spent with colleagues who are going through the same thing. Simply being reminded on a regular basis that you're not the only one who's scared, who's blocked, who's subject to despair can be an enormous relief and a first-rate block buster.

The nature of a writers' gathering—be it a course, conference, or ongoing group—has a lot to do with its value. Too many such groups are overly encouraging or needlessly discouraging. They either lend false hope to writers whose work isn't ready for publication or shatter the hopes of those who could use an encouraging word. Some of the least useful writers' groups are ones that try to be "nurturing," or "affirming," or any of the other bromides we use to try to defuse an inherently volatile situation. Those that see themselves as "support groups" too often create unrealistic expectations that are later dashed by the cold realities of publishing.

At the other end of the spectrum, an overly competitive atmosphere (like that in many academic writers' programs) can scare off promising novitiates. Writers who engage in what a scarred veteran of the Iowa Writers' Workshop called "critical karate" are prone to developing a safe, mealy-mouthed style that fends off assault by raising shields of rhetoric. Bonnie Friedman found that in response to Iowa's seminar-jousts, "It was tempting to write stories like a suit of armor, hollow but impervious to attack."

Between the poles of unearned praise and free-fire assault, it's very hard and absolutely essential for group members to seek a balance. If crippling fears are inhibiting our writing, support from a group can be invaluable. At the very least, in a candid, open group atmosphere, writers learn that they're not the only ones who are afraid. On other occasions criticism can be just as helpful. Groups provide a first line of defense: an opportunity to catch flaws in writing before they're seen by less sympathetic readers. "I have a writer's group that I depend on," said twice-published memoir writer Musa Mayer, "—not so much now for support—but to make sure I don't send something out in the world that's truly embarrassing."

A good group can foster not just courage but informed courage by helping its members cope with their fear of exposure. The best way they can do this is by requiring everyone to share work. (This has the incidental virtue of assuming that all have work to share.) In addition to sharing their writing—aloud or in manuscript—members should be expected to pay attention when others do the same. Group members don't owe each other a positive reaction. They do owe each other careful attention and candid feedback tempered by sympathy. At best, they follow the example Anne Sexton said was set by Robert Lowell: "He was never kind to the poem, he was kind to the poet." Such candor can build trust, and a sense of camaraderie. The *esprit* of a good writers' group resembles that of neighbors battling a hurricane. Everyone is in equal jeopardy. Shared danger forges a bond.

What groups, courses, and conferences provide best is a safe haven. Classmates and colleagues are stand-ins for readers—including censors in chief. Dealing with their reactions helps writers learn how to deal with those from a broader universe. If I can survive your response to my writing, perhaps I can survive my mother's.

Writers' gatherings of all kinds are, or at least ought to be, settings where we learn not so much *how* to write but how to *dare* to write. No single task is more important to the process of becoming a writer.

9

The Courageous Writer

> I have always felt that the first
> duty of a writer was to ascend—
> to make flights, carrying others
> along if he could manage it.
> To do this takes courage, even
> a certain conceit.
> —*E. B. White*

*A*fter spending more than half my life as a writer, I sometimes wonder why I'm still at it. The pay is usually spartan. Although flexible, writers' hours tend to be long. The stress level is high. Some days I have to fight pitched battles with my resolve just to get to my desk. But I've continued to write and am glad that I have. I can't think of any work I'd rather do. Some of the lowest lows of my life have come while I was writing, and some of the highest highs. Perhaps one couldn't happen without the other.

Writing and Ecstasy

Writers routinely grumble about how harrowing their life is. Ford Madox Ford—a combat veteran of World War I—

said he'd rather go through another war than face an eternity of writing novels. But Ford kept writing. So do most who get that far down the path. Despite their bellyaching, most writers say there's nothing they'd rather do, that no other activity absorbs and arouses them as writing does. "Writing is hell," said William Styron with one breath, and with the next, "I find that I'm simply the happiest, the placidest when I'm writing."

Writers commonly note this mingling of sweet and sour in their calling, its yin and yang, terror and tingle.

> Writing is allied with many splendid things— faith, inquisitiveness, and ecstasy—and with many bad things—diddling, drawing dirty pictures on the wall of public toilets, retiring from the ballgame to pick your nose in solitude. But it is, like most gifts, a paradox, and I will play my cards close to my vest and trust in the Lord.
>
> —*John Cheever*

. . . . .

> I am discomforted by the knowledge that I don't know how to write the books that I have not yet written. But that discomfort has an excitement about it, and it is the necessary antecedent of one of the best kinds of happiness.
>
> —*Wendell Berry*

. . . . .

> Why do kids play football? They can get hurt on any play, can't they? Yet they can't wait until Saturday comes around so they can play on the

high-school team, or the college team, and get
smashed around. Writing is like that. You can get
hurt, but you enjoy it.

—*Irwin Shaw*

After publishing a book of essays, a newly divorced
friend of mine became a computer programmer to support
her two children. A decade later, she still looked back on
her old vocation with nostalgia. "Writing," my friend told
me, "for all its anxiety, used to get me out of bed in the
morning. (Now I need an alarm clock and a glance at my
checkbook, and let me tell you, it's not nearly as effective.)
It was the most exciting thing I've ever done and was a
powerful antidote to all the fear. Writing has always been
the hardest work I've done but also the most fun. It's a legal
drug; the high of getting a paragraph to finally work is
unsurpassed."

The euphoria that writers experience is a reward for the
risks they take. No matter how much they dread diving into
the cold, white page, once there, writers usually find it
exhilarating. Virginia Woolf talked of "the exalted sense of
being above time and death which comes from being in a
writing mood." Many authors enter a trancelike state as
they write. Distractions disappear. Anxiety is put on hold.
After what seem like minutes, writers glance at the clock
and see that they've been working for hours. Writers often
end a working session unable to recall a word they've
written.

Those involved in daring pursuits of many kinds—
firefighting, performing, sports—typically enter a state of
hyper-concentration little different from that experienced
by writers. Athletes have a name for this state. They call it

being in "the zone." Sociologist Mihalyi Csikszentmihalyi called it a feeling of "flow." Whatever it's called, this trancelike feeling is probably due to natural opiates such as endorphins that flood our bodies when we're under stress. Such opiates induce a euphoric state of intense concentration. They also play a role in sexual arousal. That could be why writers and adventurers alike so often use sexual imagery to describe the payoff for braving danger. "Arousing," they call this feeling, "ecstatic," and even "orgiastic." Isabel Allende—who compared a blank piece of paper to a clean sheet recently ironed to make love—said that she found the process of writing so sensual, so ecstatic as to feel like an orgy. "Yet what triggers the emotion is painful," she added. "I often cry when I write."

Reaching a state of ecstasy is rarely fun for those who seek adventure. Mountaineers enjoy being at the bottom and top of a peak far more than they like being in the middle. As they begin a climb, all is hope. At the end, relief and elation take over. In between it's mostly slog and anxiety. Writers and mountain climbers share a lot in this regard. Like climbing a mountain, writing a book is exciting at the beginning, exhilarating at the end, but tedious, frustrating, and hair-raising in between. On bad days, book writers find they'd rather do anything than face their mountainous manuscript—especially during third, fourth, or twentieth drafts. At the same time, fear mounts. Danger begins to feel overwhelming. "Consciousness of it generally strikes in the night when one wakes," wrote Catherine Drinker Bowen late in her career. "Actual physical sweating takes place, loud moans are rendered, and the question is put, 'Why in God's name did one undertake such a venture, such a presumptuous, enormous, unlikely book?' "

Why indeed? Because it's there? Like high-standard mountaineering, serious writing is seldom done as a lark. These pursuits are engaged in because one is compelled to do so; because of the challenge, the self-test, to confront, engage, and transcend fear.

The joust with their own terrors lends heroism to both writers and mountain climbers. Because he could identify better with their peril, however, poet James Merrill found authors even more heroic than mountaineers. "Sir Edmund Hillary will 'do' of course," said Merrill, "but I don't gasp at his achievement the way I do at Proust's."

The Biggest Risk

Several years ago, a thirty-three-year-old sky diver named Ken Swyers tried to land on the Gateway Arch in St. Louis. His plan was to parachute from an airplane onto the six-hundred-foot arch, then leap again with a second parachute. That canopy didn't unfurl, however, and a strong wind blew Swyers down the arch leg to his death. During long conversations with his widow, sister, and friends, I tried to determine what drove this veteran sky diver to take such a risk. He had to know the odds against success were overwhelming. An answer finally emerged. Swyers—who worked on a factory assembly line—was in a state of despair. His life felt aimless. He seemed to feel that only the exhilaration and pride of doing something so risky that no one else had dared it could revive his spirits. Millie, his widow, made one more point. There were risks Kenny was ducking; ones that scared him more than leaping from airplanes with parachutes. Such as? Writing a novel, for one. This was something her husband had wanted to try.

Millie knew he wouldn't. To write fiction, he'd have had to reveal himself. That would have taken far more courage than skydiving.

When we think of "risk takers," we usually think of wire walkers, mountain climbers, and sky divers like Ken Swyers. But death-defying risks aren't necessarily the hardest ones to take. During many years of interest in this subject, it's become clear to me that the risk most universally feared is that of *looking foolish.*

Most of us would rather risk our neck than our face. One way I discovered this was by asking a number of people whether they'd leap off a high dive that scared them or climb back down past a long line of those waiting on the ladder. Most said they'd leap. On another occasion, I asked a prizefighter-turned-comedian which profession felt more dangerous. "Oh, comedy," the man said without hesitating. "By far."

"But you could die in the boxing ring," I pointed out.

"You can die up on stage," he replied. "I've seen it happen many times."

"But you get up the next morning."

"Except you don't want to."

There are many mornings when writers don't want to get up. The prospect of humiliation is just too great. Writers risk making clowns out of themselves every day of their working lives. On the fear-of-risk scale, they are engaged in a daring profession indeed. "As a writer one has to take the chance of being a fool," said Anne Sexton. "That perhaps requires the greatest courage."

Writing wouldn't be so satisfying without its sense of peril. I've often thought of finding a less anxious way to make a living than writing books (firefighting, say). But once you've climbed that mountain, other pursuits feel like strolling in foothills. "They want to write the new book," observed Malcolm Cowley about authors, "climb the new mountain, which they hope will be the highest of all, but they still regard it as only one conquest in a chain of mountains."

Many start up that mountain (or wish they could). Few reach the top. It's a rare person who's never thought, "I'd like to write a book someday." Less than one percent ever do. Some gainfully employed people explain that they'd have to take time off to write a book, a financial risk they can't dare to take. Writers regard financial risk as part of their job description, a rite of passage even. William Faulkner thought willingness to write in the face of deprivation was a test all writers had to pass. He felt that those who ducked this risk were giving themselves a vote of no confidence. "People are really afraid to find out just how much hardship and poverty they can stand," said Faulkner. "They are afraid to find out how tough they are."

To working writers whose best-sellers are yet to come, financial risk is part of the adventure. The danger of going broke arouses more than it paralyzes them. Sherwood Anderson's first publisher discovered this trait when he started sending him a weekly stipend. The publisher thought that relieving Anderson of financial uncertainty might encourage him to write more. After a few weeks, however, Anderson called off the deal. "It's no use," he explained. "I find it impossible to work with security staring me in the face."

To nonwriters, the financial insecurity of writing for a living looks daunting. From the inside, it looks different. After so many years of writing for income (or trying to, anyway), I feel recession-proof. Unemployment doesn't scare me. I've been unemployed since 1970. No one can lay me off. I've even reached the point where I rather enjoy the unpredictability of freelance writing. One never knows what the next day's mail will bring (or won't bring) in the way of a check. Knowing that there's a direct line between putting words on paper and food on the table keeps me focused: a story for a dollar. An empty bank account with the rent due can summon remarkable powers of concentration. Financial anxiety is not necessarily a downside to writing for a living. Some of the worst writing I've read was subsidized by grants, fellowships, and faculty salaries. Anthony Burgess thought the many sources of funding available to American writers actually promoted blocks because writers who didn't write for a living could better afford "the luxury of fearing the critic's pounce."

Contending with daily uncertainty keeps working writers on their toes. Past their twenties, most people's lives become rather predictable. Writers' lives don't. Taking chances is a lifelong occupation. Living on the edge makes them alert. Some days this is excruciating, other days exhilarating. Joan Didion called the writer's life one of extremes. In her words, "If you're a writer the extremes show up. They don't if you sell insurance."

A life of quiet desperation is no alternative for a working writer. To write well, they must risk themselves, and always in public. The one risk a working writer doesn't run is of slipping into a safe, monotonous dotage.

No Regrets

I often meet people who lament—sometimes bitterly— their choice of career. I've rarely met any writers who felt this way. They may wish they'd written better; that's almost a given. Or that their publisher paid better attention to their books. Or that more readers had bought them. But as for choosing to risk writing, most were proud.

Regrets are usually greater for risks avoided than for those taken—even ones taken and lost. Daring to write is more satisfying than ducking that risk regardless of whether we get the hoped-for results. And success or failure aren't the only possible outcomes of daring to write. In the process, we may find we're better suited to one type of writing than another; essays, say, instead of short stories. Or we may realize our aspirations need adjustment: from producing the Great American Novel to writing one we're proud of. While trying to get published in well-known magazines, we may discover quality publications we didn't know existed. As a last resort, we can follow in the footsteps of Whitman, Poe, and Twain to publish our own work.

Too many talented writers give up too soon. They may have taken a stab at writing, sent some work out, only to find rejections got them discouraged. One retiree told me that she never wrote another word after her short story came in second to one by William Saroyan in a young writers' contest. Instead she got a master's degree and made social work her career. Now in her late seventies, this woman wondered if she'd made a mistake.

I've met many like her who abandoned an early dream of becoming a writer only to mourn this decision late in a life lived more "realistically." As we've seen, there's no shortage of good reasons not to write. But many are simply disguises for timidity. There's much to be said for not doing what we most want to do. If we fail at something we don't care about, so what? Little was at stake. Aspiring only to second-place goals is a first-rate way to hedge our bets. Among the least appreciated reasons for doing superficial, second-rate work of any kind is the comfort of knowing that it's not our best that's on the line. Far more is at risk when we do what we really *want* to do rather than something less. I don't think we'll ever fully appreciate the role of not daring to risk a shattered dream in limiting people to second-choice careers and third-choice lives.

The Branwell Brontë Syndrome

Think of this as the Branwell Brontë syndrome. Branwell Brontë spent years hanging around pubs talking about the great novel he was going to write. At the age of thirty-one he took sick and died. Branwell may have been the most gifted Bronte of all. His sisters thought he was. The rest of us will never know. Branwell never showed his novel fragments to a publisher. When asked why, he said he couldn't bear the thought of a contemptuous editor throwing his work into the fire. Branwell's three sisters, though perhaps not as gifted as their brother, actually wrote, mailed their writing, and got it published. Their names—Charlotte, Emily, and Anne Brontë—are the ones we remember.

In writing, as in so many pursuits, it's not the most gifted but the most determined who succeed. John Berryman thought talent was no more than twenty percent of a successful poet's makeup. This is probably true for any type of writer. Those we hear about are more blessed with pluck and persistence than ability and skill. According to Thomas McGuane, the most successful members of his writing program at Stanford—himself, Larry McMurtry, Ken Kesey—were not the most gifted ones; only the most willful. "Kesey was not even remotely the best writer in class," said McGuane of the author of *One Flew Over the Cuckoo's Nest*, "but he was maniacally determined."

Writing teachers routinely observe that their best students are seldom the ones whose byline they see in later years. Those who wowed the class with dazzling powers of expression usually sink from sight. W. D. Snodgrass—who taught Anne Sexton at the Antioch Writers' Conference—later said that several of her classmates were better poets than she. None were as driven. Early in her career Sexton began keeping a log in which she recorded when poems went out and when they came back. According to that log, Sexton remailed any rejected poem within days. This meant that she sometimes submitted the same poem to different magazines up to fifteen times a year. As biographer Diane Middlebrook points out, such persistence would be remarkable in a writer at any level of experience, let alone one just getting started.

Like teachers, editors find that the writers they publish most often are seldom the best ones. Brilliant writers tend to have trouble producing publishable material on a regular basis. "There are a lot of talented people who are very erratic," said Gloria Steinem, when she was editing *Ms.*, "so either they don't turn [an article] in or they turn it in and it's rotten; it's amazing. Somebody who's even maybe not all that terrific but who is dependable, who will turn in a publishable piece more or less on time, can really do very well."

I'm often asked whether, with so many people jostling to publish, there's room for one more. My answer is yes; there is always room for another writer who is gifted enough to compose readable material and reliable enough to keep that material coming. I sometimes add—only semifacetiously—that editors won't hold it against writers if they're brilliant, but would really rather they weren't. What editors prefer is someone who can turn in a good piece of writing close to the date promised. If the piece is inspired, that's a bonus.

When I try to make this point to aspiring writers, eyes glaze over all around the room. And I know the thoughts behind those glazed eyes: "This guy hasn't got a clue about how brilliant I am. Can't he recognize true genius when it's sitting right in front of him? I'll show him." My response is: "Great! Show me. Your determination to put me in my place will take you a lot farther than your genius."

When it comes to publishing on a regular basis, brilliance and erudition are basically beside the point. That's a hard truth for talented writers to assimilate. They're not lacking in ability or skills. Many are well versed in the literary arts. Where they come up short is in being able to confront the curious blend of terror and tedium that working writers deal with every day. "Talent is extremely common," said Kurt Vonnegut. "What is rare is the willingness to endure the life of a writer. It is like making wallpaper by hand for the Sistine Chapel."

Writers talk little about talent and admire it even less. Any writer knows dozens more who are just as able, if not more so, but who now write only in their journal, if they write at all. "They can't take the ridicule," said Norman Mailer of such gifted flameouts. According to Mailer, his Brooklyn high school was filled with better writers than he. Mailer didn't even try out for the school literary magazine. Only after enrolling at Harvard did he begin to write in earnest. Even then, Mailer admitted, "My teachers thought

I was fair, but I don't believe they ever thought for a moment that I was really talented."

Writers like Mailer push on in the face of reason and despite the most daunting obstacles. Far from being driven by inspiration, most working writers are distinguished by a high tolerance for boredom and an exaggerated fear of the consequences should they stop putting words on paper. The real terror for such a writer involves having to take a day job with set hours and a supervisor; being forced to return a publisher's advance and confess that he couldn't finish a project; feeling revealed as a fraud who said he could write a book but couldn't; admitting that he doesn't have what it takes after all. Like most working writers, I'm sometimes complimented on my self-discipline: the fact that I go to my desk every morning to write. That's not the way it feels to me. What I'm usually feeling is apprehensive—that if I don't go to my desk and stay there for a few hours recording words on paper, I may have to get a real job with a real boss and real hours and dress requirements.

On the one hand, this profile of the working writer sounds dull; unromantic. It's not Jane Fonda playing Lillian Hellman, emoting and smoking as she pounds out Great American Plays in the movie *Julia.* If you imagine yourself to be a budding Fonda–Hellman, or possibly even a Tolstoy, it's not a pretty picture. If, on the other hand, you think of yourself as smart enough, gifted even, and reasonably self-disciplined, it could be seen as encouraging. That's how I prefer to look at it. Success as a writer is within the grasp of whoever can tell a story on paper that people want to hear, *and* is willing to persist, to put up with boredom, frustration, and anxiety. Determined writers will find ways to get published regardless of whether they are brilliant or have a degree from the Iowa Writers' Workshop.

The most understandable trap is to wait for fear to subside before starting one's journey. It doesn't, won't, and shouldn't. Too much good writing comes from writers on the edge. Trying to defeat or portage around normal writing anxieties merely postpones the day when we confront our fears directly and find the courage to write. "Once we are aware of our fears, we are almost always capable of being more courageous than we think," wrote Lawrence Block. "Someone once told me that fear and courage are like lightning and thunder; they both start out at the same time, but the fear travels faster and arrives sooner. If we just wait a moment, the requisite courage will be along shortly."

Courage Boosters

None of this is to say that it doesn't help to be well equipped. But writing aids must be chosen carefully, with an eye to what's actually helpful. In an earlier chapter I wrote about "false fear busters" (new gear, a better office, good agent, etc.). Now let's look at some genuine courage boosters:

- read about successful writers, paying attention to *their* fears and how they dealt with them
- take a writing course or two
- attend an occasional writers' conference
- join a serious writers' group
- develop anxiety-easing rituals, no matter how eccentric

- devise fear-taming work techniques, no matter how gimmicky
- write at times of day when you're most productive and least anxious
- identify your censor in chief and mentally rehearse how to deal with that person
- get to know yourself well enough not to be too terrified by what escapes from within onto the page
- convert fear into excitement
- write

Since fears are so singular among writers, it's hard to suggest specific antidotes suited to them all. Part of a writer's challenge is to identify inhibiting anxieties and devise ways to keep them from turning into blocks. Tactics I've found useful over the years include: engaging only in "just-in-time worrying," trying not to obsess about a manuscript until there's simply no alternative; when possible, not writing or even thinking about writing past sundown; never, *ever* fretting about a project as I'm trying to go to sleep (this contributes nothing to one's manuscript but does make it harder to work on it the next day); decreasing the amount of time I spend preparing to write, and increasing the amount I spend writing. Among other things, starting to write before I feel ready makes me realize how much of the research I planned to do was unnecessary.

Setting Sail

Up to a point, preparation can ease the fears of those setting out on the writer's journey. Beyond that point, planning enhances anxiety. Wisdom resides in knowing how much planning to do and when the time has come to push off from shore. That's where courage is called for. Help can be sought from those who have already made the trip. Let's say I'm someone who's sailed solo across the Atlantic. You can come to me for advice on how to make the same voyage. I can give you a map. We can discuss currents and weather conditions and what provisions you'll need. I can even help you build a boat strong enough to survive rough waters. But *you* must push off from shore. No one else can do that.

The same thing is true about writing. At some point we must stop anticipating our journey and set sail. Willa Cather said that she wrote best when she stopped trying to write and began simply to *remember*. Many of her colleagues have discovered the same thing. Once we forget we're *writing*, we're freer to *write*. That's one reason writers resort to so many gimmicks: to trick themselves out of realizing they're writing.

There are very few "writing problems," as such; only human ones. A lot of what we take to be writing problems are really courage problems, problems about being honest, confronting others and confronting our selves. We work so hard on our writing when we really should be working on our will. We're all better writers when we worry more about what we want to say and less about how it sounds. I've sometimes thought I'd help students most by not teaching "writing" at all. Rather, I'd try to help them take more risks, find more courage, learn to deal better with Important Others, and—especially—with themselves. E. B. White thought that the writer's key problem was to establish communication with himself. Once that was accomplished, he said, "everyone else is tuned in. In other words, if a writer succeeds in communicating with a reader, I think it is simply because he has been trying (with some success) to get in touch with himself."

All of us might like to explore our inner lives with the courage of a White, a Proust, or a Dove. We enjoy reading such authors' work—and admire them so much—both because of their valor and because of what we can learn about ourselves by their example. In the process, writers and readers forge a unique bond. Rita Dove said that writing poems not only helped her understand herself but also helped her connect with others. As Dove put it, "The final thing is, if someone else can come up to me and say, 'I know exactly what you mean,' or 'That happened to me, too,' or 'You know, that could have been my grandmother' . . . that is the final thrill of writing."

Even though writing is a solo trek, writers are never alone. The reader is always at their side. Discovering that is one of the most pleasant and unexpected dividends of this adventure. Something I never realized until I became a writer is the confidential relationship author and reader enjoy. Writers can discuss things with readers that might be difficult to talk about in person. They, in turn, can respond from their private thoughts, with no need to speak a word. If the writer's honesty feels embarrassing, the reader's forgiveness is profound. On occasion I'll meet a reader, usually with pleasure. We shared a perilous journey.

Notes

Published or broadcast sources of information are cited in these notes. Where none is cited, the author's source was a personal interview or conversation.

1. Writing as an Act of Courage

3   Ozick: *New York Times Book Review*, February 6, 1983, 11.

White's rewriting: Beverly Gherman, *E. B. White: Some Writer!* (New York: Atheneum, 1992), 103.

Writers Not *at Work*: Dorothy Lobrano Guth, ed., *Letters of E. B. White* (New York: Harper and Row, 1976), 449.

4   "The second most inactive writer living": Scott Elledge, *E. B. White: A Biography* (New York: Norton, 1984), 205.

Dartmouth episode: Guth, *Letters*, 295.

Childhood fears: George Plimpton, ed., *Writers at Work*, 8th ser. (New York: Viking, 1988), 6.

Youthful fears: Elledge, *E. B. White*, 63.

"Much of the story": Elledge, *E. B. White*, 23.

5   Epstein: Joseph Epstein, *Partial Payments* (New York: Norton, 1989), 308.

"The Second Tree from the Corner": E. B. White, *The Second Tree from the Corner* (New York: Harper and Brothers, 1954), 97–103.

"I am not inclined": Guth, *Letters*, 485.

"A writer's courage": *The National Book Award: Writers on Their Craft and Their World* (New York: Book-of-the-Month, 1990), 52.

6   "I admire anybody": Plimpton, *Writers at Work*, 8th ser., 11.

Cheever: John Cheever, *The Journals of John Cheever* (New York: Knopf, 1991), x.

Porter: George Plimpton, ed., *Writers at Work*, 2d ser. (New York: Viking, 1963), 149.

8   Ashbery: Donald M. Murray, *Shoptalk: Learning to Write with Writers* (Portsmouth, N.H.: Boynton/Cook, 1990), 94.

Cowley: George Plimpton, ed., *Writers at Work*, 1st ser. (New York: Viking, 1958), 14.

Baldwin: Murray, *Shoptalk*, 94.

Poll of fears: R. H. Bruskin, *The Bruskin Report*, July 1973, 1–2.

9   Atwood: Janet Sternburg, *The Writer on Her Work*, vol. 2 (New York: Norton, 1991), 152.

Ozick: Sybil Steinberg, ed., *Writing for Your Life* (Wainscott, N.Y.: Pushcart Press, 1992), 387.

11   Friedman: Bonnie Friedman, *Writing Past Dark* (New York: HarperCollins, 1993), 56.

13   Twain: Mark Twain, *Pudd'nhead Wilson* (1894), in Bernard DeVoto, ed., *The Portable Mark Twain* (1946; reprint, New York: Viking, 1968), 559.

Bradley: *The American Weekly*, November 7, 1954, 2.

May: Rollo May, *The Courage to Create* (New York: Norton, 1975; New York: Bantam, 1976), 3.

Barth: George Plimpton, ed., *Writers at Work*, 7th ser. (New York: Viking, 1986), 233.

15   Murray: Murray, *Shoptalk*, 25.

2. Points of Courage

16   Kosinski: George Plimpton, ed., *Writers at Work*, 5th ser. (New York: Viking, 1981), 329.

18   Godwin: Janet Sternburg, *The Writer on Her Work*, vol. 1 (New York: Norton, 1980), 252.

19   Allende: "On Creativity: A Special Program on Women and

Writing," Grace Cathedral, San Francisco, broadcast on WYSO radio, Yellow Springs, Ohio, September 2, 1994.

Gurney: *Christian Science Monitor*, January 23, 1989.

20 Miller: Donald M. Murray, *Shoptalk: Learning to Write with Writers* (Portsmouth, N.H.: Boynton/Cook, 1990), 39.

24 Marquez: Murray, *Shoptalk*, 75.

Lebowitz: Jon Winokur, *Writers on Writing* (Philadelphia: Running Press, 1987), 120.

Steinbeck: Murray, *Shoptalk*, 125.

25 Atwood: Joyce Carol Oates, ed., *First Person Singular: Writers on Their Craft* (Princeton, N.J.: Ontario Review Press, 1983), 89.

Dunbar: Glynne Robinson Betts, *Writers-in-Residence: American Authors at Home* (New York: Viking, 1981), 120.

Burgess: *New York Times*, April 12, 1981.

Wolfe: Murray, *Shoptalk*, 77.

26 Dillard: Annie Dillard, *The Writing Life* (New York: Harper and Row, 1989), 52.

Conroy: *Chicago Tribune*, November 25, 1986.

Jones: Willie Morris, *James Jones: A Friendship* (Garden City, N.Y.: Doubleday, 1978), 107.

27 Murdoch: Sternburg, *The Writer on Her Work*, vol. 1, 252.

Faulkner: George Plimpton, ed., *Writers at Work*, 1st ser. (New York: Viking, 1958), 123.

28 Valéry: W. H. Auden, *A Certain World* (New York: Viking, 1970), 423.

29 Heinlein: *Analog*, January 1974, 7.

Morrison: Claudia Tate, ed., *Black Women Writers at Work* (New York: Continuum, 1986), 131.

King: Larry L. King, *None But a Blockhead* (New York: Viking, 1986), 46.

30 Trollope: Park Honan, *Author's Lives* (New York: St. Martin's, 1990), 30; Winokur, *Writers on Writing*, 125.

32 Welty: George Plimpton, ed., *Writers at Work*, 4th ser. (New York: Viking, 1976), 275.

Durrell: George Plimpton, ed., *Writers at Work*, 2d ser. (New York: Viking, 1963), 270.

Stark: Larry Dark, ed., *Literary Outtakes* (New York: Fawcett, 1990), 275–76.

33 Allen: Clifton Fadiman, ed., *The Little, Brown Book of Anecdotes* (Boston: Little, Brown, 1985), 15.

34 Irving: Donald Hall, ed., *The Oxford Book of American Literary Anecdotes* (New York: Oxford University Press, 1981), 34–35.

35 Melville: *New York Times*, April 12, 1985.
Malamud, Updike: *New York Times*, January 4, 1983.
O'Hara: Hall, *American Literary Anecdotes*, 300–301.
James: *Parade*, August 1, 1982, 16.

36 Gertler: *New York Times*, June 14, 1984.

37 Marek: *Publishers Weekly*, April 17, 1987, 39.
Deval: *Publishers Weekly*, November 15, 1993, 35.

3. Will Everyone See Through Me?

38 Rostand: Meic Stephens, *A Dictionary of Literary Quotations* (London: Routledge, 1990), 79.
Conroy: *People*, February 2, 1981, 67–69; *Publishers Weekly*, June 20, 1986, 30; *Chicago Tribune*, November 25, 1986; *Atlanta*, September 1991, 56–59, 139–42; December 1991, 7; *San Francisco Focus*, December 1991, 76–83, 100–101, 149; *Los Angeles Times*, December 26, 1991.

39 Millay: Stephens, *Literary Quotations*, 120.
White: Dorothy Lobrano Guth, ed., *Letters of E. B. White* (New York: Harper and Row, 1976), 516, 655.

40 Galbraith: Donald M. Murray, *Shoptalk: Learning to Write with Writers* (Portsmouth, N.H.: Boynton/Cook, 1990), 73.

42 Ueland: Brenda Ueland, *If You Want to Write* (1938; reprint, St. Paul, Minn.: Schubert Club, 1984), 91.
Roth: Philip Roth, *The Counterlife* (New York: Farrar Straus Giroux, 1986), 127.

43 Dillard: Annie Dillard, *The Writing Life* (New York: Harper and Row, 1989), 68.

Gordimer: Susan Stamberg, *Talk* (New York: Random House, 1993), 132.

Busch: Nicholas Delbanco and Laurence Goldstein, ed., *Writers and Their Craft: Short Stories and Essays on the Narrative* (Detroit: Wayne State University Press, 1991), 98.

Dove: "After Reading *Mickey in the Night Kitchen* for the Third Time Before Bed," in Rita Dove, *Grace Notes* (New York: Norton, 1989), 41.

46 Zinsser: William Zinsser, ed., *Inventing the Truth: The Art and Craft of Memoir* (Boston: Houghton Mifflin, 1987), 16–17.

47 Strasberg: *Publisher's Weekly*, May 2, 1980, 16.

Fowles: *The Sunday Telegraph*, February 9, 1992.

48 Ginsberg: George Plimpton, ed., *Writers at Work*, 3d ser. (New York: Viking, 1963), 287.

Jong: *New York Times Book Review*, August 16, 1981, 20.

Gurney: A. R. Gurney, *The Cocktail Hour* (New York: Plume, 1990), 29, 43, 41; *Time*, October 31, 1988, 85; *People*, January 23, 1989, 103–4; *Washington Times*, August 29, 1989; *Los Angeles Times*, May 9, 1991.

50 Taylor: Sybil Steinberg, ed., *Writing for Your Life* (Wainscott, N.Y.: Pushcart Press, 1992), 495.

Carver: WPTD TV, Dayton, Ohio, September 24, 1993, broadcast of documentary about Carver, KCTS TV, Seattle, Wash., 1992.

Conroy: *Louisville Courier-Journal*, November 19, 1989; *Los Angeles Times*, December 26, 1991; *Phoenix Gazette*, July 22, 1994; *Dayton Daily News*, July 29, 1994.

51 Godwin: Janet Sternburg, *The Writers on Her Work*, vol. 1 (New York: Norton, 1980), 252.

Roth: Roth, *The Counterlife*, 208, 205; Philip Roth, *The Anatomy Lesson* (New York: Farrar Straus Giroux, 1983), 58.

53 Stamberg, Roth: Stamberg, *Talk*, 208–9.

Braudy: Bill Gordon, *"How Many Books Do You Sell in Ohio?"* (Akron, Ohio: North Ridge Books, 1986), 137.

Roiphe: Susan Shaughnessy, *Walking on Alligators: A Book of Meditations for Writers* (New York: HarperCollins, 1993), 34.

Greene: Murray, *Shoptalk*, 85.

54 Wolff, Carver: WPTD TV, September 24, 1993.

55 Didion: Joan Didion *Slouching Towards Bethlehem* (New York: Farrar, Straus & Giroux, 1968; New York: Washington Square Press, 1981), 14.

Greene: Graham Greene, *A Sort of Life* (London: Bodley Head, 1971; Middlesex, England: Penguin, 1972), 134.

de Maupassant: Murray, *Shoptalk*, 19.

Bennett: James Sutherland, ed., *The Oxford Book of Literary Anecdotes* (Oxford: Clarendon Press, 1975), 321.

56 Cather: James Woodress, *Willa Cather: A Literary Life* (Lincoln, Nebr.: University of Nebraska Press, 1987), 191, 531; Donald Hall, ed., *The Oxford Book of American Literary Anecdotes* (New York: Oxford University Press, 1981), 159.

Faulkner: George Plimpton, ed., *Writers at Work*, 1st ser. (New York: Viking, 1958), 124.

57 Lowell, Spender: George Plimpton, ed., *Writers at Work*, 6th ser. (New York: Viking, 1984), 72.

Didion: *Los Angeles Times*, May 9, 1971.

Connolly: Cyril Connolly, *Enemies of Promise* (1938; reprint, New York: Macmillan, 1948), 116.

Kesey: James Charlton, ed., *The Writer's Quotation Book* (Wainscott, N.Y.: Pushcart Press, 1991), 60; *Time*, May 24, 1982, 79.

O'Neill: *New York Times Book Review*, August 16, 1981, 20.

Humphrey: Steinberg, *Writing for Your Life*, 276.

58 Mailer: Plimpton, *Writers at Work*, 3rd ser., 268.

Rorem: Joyce Carol Oates, ed., *First Person Singular: Writers on Their Craft* (Princeton, N.J.: Ontario Review Press, 1983), 95.

Dove: interviewed on WYSO radio, Yellow Springs, Ohio, February 16, 1994.

59 Robbins: *People*, July 2, 1990, 110.

Allende: *All Things Considered*, National Public Radio, June 12, 1993; interviewed on WYSO radio, February 18, 1994.

Benedict: Jon Winokur, *Writers on Writing* (Philadelphia: Running Press, 1987), 86.

60 Jong: *New York Times Book Review*, August 16, 1981, 20.

Marriott: Michel Marriott, *Essence*, November 1990, 73–74, 115–16.

61 Tan: *USA Today*, October 5, 1993.

Updike: *New York Times Book Review*, August 16, 1981, 20.

Conroy: *Chicago Tribune*, November 25, 1986; September 5, 1986, 86; *St. Petersburg Times*, July 6, 1990; *Atlanta*, September 1991, 58; December 1991, 7; *San Francisco Focus*, December 1991, 80; *Los Angeles Times*, December 26, 1991.

4. The Devil in the Inkstand

64 Jong: Susan Shaughnessy, *Walking on Alligators: A Book of Meditation for Writers* (New York: HarperCollins, 1993), 5.

"A guilty, addictive thrill": *The New Yorker*, July 26, 1993, 89.

66 Faulkner: William Faulkner, *Mosquitoes* (1927; reprint, New York: Liveright, 1955), 251.

67 Melville: "Herman Melville: Damned in Paradise," documentary film, The Film Company, Washington, D.C., 1985.

Busch: *New York Times Book Review*, August 18, 1991, 6.

68 Unemployed executive: *New York Times*, May 31, 1977.

69 Frost: Elaine Barry, *Robert Frost on Writing* (New Brunswick, N.J.: Rutgers University Press, 1973), 126.

Dove: *Bill Moyers' Journal*, PBS Television, April 2, 1994.

70 Cheever: *New York Times*, December 3, 1985.

Updike: Jon Winokur, *Writers on Writing* (Philadelphia: Running Press, 1987), 44.

Conroy: Pat Conroy, *The Great Santini* (Boston: Houghton Mifflin, 1976), 147–48; *San Francisco Focus*, December 1991, 81.

72 Johnson: *New York Times Book Review*, September 16, 1979, 1.

Doctorow: Tom LeClair and Larry McCaffery, ed., *Anything Can Happen: Interviews with Contemporary American Novelists* (Urbana, Ill.: University of Illinois Press, 1983), 105.

73 Hemingway: Ernest Hemingway, *Death in the Afternoon* (New York: Scribner's, 1932), 2.

Flanner: Brenda Wineapple, *Genêt: A Biography of Janet Flanner* (New York: Ticknor and Fields, 1989), 104, 107–8, 208–9.

74 Hawthorne: George Plimpton, ed., *Writers at Work*, 1st ser. (New York: Viking, 1958), 17.

Welty: George Plimpton, ed., *Writers at Work*, 4th ser. (New York: Viking, 1976), 275.

Hersey: George Plimpton, ed., *Writers at Work*, 8th ser. (New York: Viking, 1988), 126.

75 Bellow: Donald M. Murray, *Shoptalk: Learning to Write with Writers* (Portsmouth, N.H.: Boynton/Cook, 1990), 36.

Miller: *Los Angeles Times WEST*, January 23, 1972, 20.

76 Wolfelike writer: Richard Ben Cramer, *What it Takes* (New York: Random House, 1992), 30.

77 Tyrrell: R. Emmett Tyrrell, Jr., *The American Spectator*, July 1979, 4.

78 Homeless New Yorker: *New York Times*, October 26, 1985.

Gass: Winokur, *Writers on Writing*, 16.

79 Mencken: H. L. Mencken, *A Mencken Chrestomathy* (New York: Knopf, 1949), 466.

Durrell: George Plimpton, ed., *Writers at Work*, 2d ser. (New York: Viking, 1963), 273.

White: *The New Yorker*, December 27, 1993–January 3, 1994, 103; E. B. White, *Essays of E. B. White* (New York: Harper and Row, 1977; New York: Harper Colophon, 1979), viii.

80 Frost: Plimpton, *Writers at Work*, 2d ser., 42.

Frost, MacLeish: David Haward Bain and Mary Smyth Duffy, ed., *Whose Woods These Are: A History of the Bread Loaf Writer's Conference, 1926–1992* (New York: Ecco, 1993), 40–41; Wallace Stegner, *The Uneasy Chair: A Biography of Bernard DeVoto* (Garden City, N.Y.: Doubleday, 1974), 205–6, 424.

81 Johnson, Samuel Johnson, *The Rambler*, W. J. Bate and Albrecht B. Strauss, ed., (New Haven, Conn.: Yale University Press, 1969), 13.

Jones: George Plimpton, ed., *Writers at Work*, 3d ser. (New York: Viking, 1967), 250.

Orwell: Sonia Orwell and Jan Angus, ed., *The Collected Essays, Journalism, and Letters of George Orwell* (New York: Harcourt, Brace and World, 1968), 3.

Geisel: *Time*, August 11, 1967, 59; *Reader's Digest*, April 1972, 143; *Providence Journal-Bulletin*, September 3, 1987.

Kennedy: *New York Times*, May 11, 1984.

82 Hillerman: Sybil Steinberg, ed., *Writing for Your Life* (Wainscott, N.Y.: Pushcart Press, 1992), 267; *Los Angeles Times*, January 2, 1981.

Amis: George Plimpton, ed., *Writers at Work*, 5th ser. (New York: Viking, 1981), 185.

Keillor: running theme on *Prairie Home Companion*, American Public Radio.

Kizer: *USA Today*, June 23, 1989.

Ferber: James Charlton, ed., *The Writer's Quotation Book* (Wainscott, N.Y.: Pushcart Press, 1991), 82.

83 Gass: Plimpton, *Writers at Work*, 5th ser., 284–85.

Edel: Leon Edel, *Stuff of Sleep and Dreams* (New York: Harper and Row, 1982), 94.

Grisham: Shaughnessy, *Walking on Alligators*, 172.

Grafton: *Publishers Weekly*, May 5, 1989, 39.

King: speech to National Press Club, WYSO radio, Yellow Springs, Ohio, October 28, 1993.

84 McMurtry: *Los Angeles Times*, February 17, 1972.

King: *New Times*, November 16, 1973, 27.

Coleridge: James Sutherland, ed., *The Oxford Book of Literary Anecdotes* (Oxford: Clarendon Press, 1975), 154.

Orwell: Orwell and Angus, *Collected Essays*, 1.

85 Munro: Alice Munro, *Lives of Girls and Women* (New York: McGraw-Hill, 1971; New York: Signet, 1974), 206.

Cukor: *New York*, February 16, 1976, 35.

86 Thoreau: Joyce Carol Oates, ed., *First Person Singular: Writers on Their Craft* (Princeton, N.J.: Ontario Review Press, 1983), 52.

Mencken, Lewis: Donald Hall, ed., *The Oxford Book of American Literary Anecdotes* (New York: Oxford University Press, 1981), 203.

87   Exley: Winokur, *Writers on Writing*, 121; Geoffrey Wolff, *Los Angeles Times Book Review*, May 4, 1975; Fredick Exley, *A Fan's Notes* (New York: Harper and Row, 1968), 45–46.

89   Vonnegut: *Time*, March 3, 1969, 79.

Hazzard: *New York Times*, March 26, 1980.

5. Finessing Fear

93   Voltaire: Edward Latham, *Famous Sayings and Their Authors* (1904; reprint, Detroit: Gale, 1970), 131.

Block: Lawrence Block, *Write for Your Life* (Fort Myers, Fla.: Lawrence Block, 1986), 38–39, 42.

94   Wolfe: *New York Times*, April 12, 1981.

96   Hemingway: Ernest Hemingway, *A Moveable Feast* (New York: Scribner's, 1964), 73–75; Jeffrey Meyers, *Hemingway: A Biography* (New York: Harper and Row, 1985), 68–70; Alice Hunt Sokoloff, *Hadley: The First Mrs. Hemingway* (New York: Dodd, Mead, 1973), 58–60; *Dayton Daily News*, July 17, 1992.

Lawrence: Nicholas Parsons, ed., *The Book of Literary Lists* (New York: Facts on File, 1987), 63.

97   Carlyle: James Sutherland, ed., *The Oxford Book of Literary Anecdotes* (Oxford, Clarendon Press, 1975), 204–5; Parsons, *Literary Lists*, 61–62.

Godwin: Janet Sternburg, *The Writer on Her Work*, vol. 1 (New York: Norton, 1980), 245.

Kingston: *Newsweek*, November 4, 1991, 35.

Steinbeck, Konitz: Robert Hendrickson, *The Literary Life and Other Curiosities* (New York: Viking, 1981), 14–15.

98   Tyler: *New York Times Book Review*, February 6, 1983, 24.

Tan: Mickey Pearlman and Katherine Usher Henderson, ed., *Inter/View: Talks with America's Writing Women* (Lexington, Ky.: University Press of Kentucky, 1990), 21.

99   Fox: *Journal of Medical Education*, 48 (1973), 630–35.

100   Yevtushenko: *Christian Science Monitor*, March 8, 1991.

101   Jerrold: Sutherland, *Literary Anecdotes*, 243; Clifton Fadiman, ed., *The Little, Brown Book of Anecdotes* (Boston: Little, Brown, 1985), 81, 308.

102   Stein: Gertrude Stein, *Tender Buttons* (1914; reprint, New York: Haskell House, 1970), 13, 24.

      Stein, Cerf: Bennett Cerf, *At Random* (New York: Random House, 1977), 103.

103   Hampl: Brenda Ueland, *If You Want to Write* (1938; reprint, St. Paul, Minn.: Schubert Club, 1984), x.

      Teradyne report: William Lutz, *Doublespeak* (New York: Harper and Row, 1989; New York: HarperPerennial, 1990), 120.

      Robinson: Jill Robinson, *Bed/Time/Story* (New York: Random House, 1974; New York: Fawcett Crest, 1975), 13.

104   Editor, Oates: *Philadelphia Inquirer*, September 21, 1982.

      Researcher: *New York*, October 24, 1988, 37.

      Gowers: Sir Ernest Gowers, *Plain Words: Their ABC* (New York: Knopf, 1954), 146.

105   Eisenhower: Steve Neal, *The Eisenhowers* (Garden City, N.Y.: Doubleday, 1978), 24, 72, 76; *Los Angeles Times*, June 13, 1972.

      Masters and Johnson: Paul Robinson, *The Modernization of Sex* (New York: Harper and Row, 1976), 123–25.

107   Truman: Harry S. Truman, *Memoirs. Vol. 2: Years of Trial and Hope* (Garden City, N.Y.: Doubleday, 1956), 1.

      Truman: William Hillman, *Mr. President* (New York: Farrar Straus Young, 1952), 143.

108   "A multi-purpose thrust": *Philadelphia Inquirer*, April 22, 1979.

      "The functional methodology": Mario Pei, *Double-Speak in America* (New York: Hawthorn, 1973), 66.

109   Systematic study: *College English*, 43 (September 1981), 433–51.

110   Armstrong: *INTERFACES*, 10 (1980), 80–86; *Psychology Today*, May 1980, 12.

111   Limerick: *New York Times Book Review*, October 31, 1993, 3, 23–24.

Hemingway: Hemingway, *A Movable Feast*, 17–18.

112   Darwin: Donald M. Murray, *A Writer Teaches Writing: A Practical Method of Teaching Composition* (Boston: Houghton Mifflin, 1968), 234.

Cutter Insect Repellent, circa 1972.

113   White: George Plimpton, ed., *Writers at Work*, 8th ser. (New York: Viking, 1988), 20.

Twain: Mark Twain, "Simplified Spelling," speech, 1906, in Charles Neider, ed., *Plymouth Rock and the Pilgrims and Other Salutory Platform Opinions* (New York: Harper and Row, 1984), 267.

114   Churchill: *Churchill: In Memoriam*, written and edited by the staff of the *New York Times* (New York: Bantam, 1965), 160.

Prelutsky: *Los Angeles Times WEST*, September 7, 1969.

Moskowitz: Faye Moskowitz, *A Leak in the Heart* (Boston: David Godine, 1985), 26.

115   Porter: George Plimpton, ed., *Writers at Work*, 2d ser. (New York: Viking, 1963), 156.

116   Redd: *Dayton Daily News*, March 31, 1993.

6. Putting Fear to Work

120   Frankel: *Adweek*, February 6, 1984, CR-30.

Didion: *Ms.*, February 1977, 68, 108; *Writer's Digest*, February 1974, 6; Sara Davidson, *New York Times Book Review*, April 3, 1977, 35; *New York Times Magazine*, June 10, 1979, 38, 40; *New York Times Book Review*, December 5, 1976, 2; George Plimpton, ed., *Writers at Work*, 5th ser. (New York: Viking, 1981), 354.

121   Dickey: *New York Times Magazine*, June 10, 1979, 35.

Steinem: *LA*, October 28, 1972, 6.

Kazin: *Harper's*, December 1971, 122, 116. \

122   Grossman: Susan Shaughnessy, *Walking on Alligators: A Book of Meditations for Writers* (New York: HarperCollins, 1993), 124.

Brown: Mickey Pearlman and Katherine Usher Henderson, ed., *Inter/View: Talks with America's Writing Women* (Lexington, Ky.: University Press of Kentucky, 1990), 106.

Bowen: *Atlantic Monthly*, December 1957, 87.

123   White: Donald M. Murray, *Shoptalk: Learning to Write with Writers* (Portsmouth, N.H.: Boynton/Cook, 1990), 66.

McKain: *Washington Post*, October 9, 1990; Thomas L. McKain and Carol R. Glass, "Cognitive and Behavioral Factors in Writing Anxiety," undated.

124   Burke: Kenneth Burke, *Counter-Statement* (New York: Harcourt Brace, 1931), 95.

Valenzuela: Janet Sternburg *The Writer on Her Work*, vol. 2 (New York: Norton, 1991), 193.

Dove: *Newsday*, November 29, 1992.

125   Jong: *Los Angeles Times*, November 24, 1974.

Fenichel: *International Journal of Psychoanalysis*, 20 (1939), 263–74.

Picasso: Francois Gilot and Carlton Lake, *Life with Picasso* (New York: McGraw-Hill, 1964; New York: Penguin, 1966), 257.

West: Jessamyn West, *Hide and Seek* (New York: Harcourt Brace Jovanovich), 237.

126   Chandler: Frank MacShane, ed., *Selected Letters of Raymond Chandler* (New York: Dell, 1987), 443; Frank MacShane, *The Life of Raymond Chandler* (New York: Dutton, 1976), 73, 50, 29, 59; Raymond Chandler, *The Midnight Raymond Chandler* (Boston: Houghton Mifflin, 1971), 7.

127   Auster: Sybil Steinberg, ed., *Writing for Your Life* (Wainscott, N.Y.: Pushcart Press, 1992), 38.

Morrison: *Washington Post*, October 5, 1987.

129   Stone: Charles Ruas, *Conversations with American Writers* (New York: Knopf, 1985), 287.

Moreau: *New Yorker*, March 13, 1978, 46.

130   D'Amato: Channel 5 News, New York, December 14, 1990; *Dayton Daily News*, December 18, 1990.

Torres: *Village Voice*, May 6–12, 1981, 22.

131 Didion: *New York Times Book Review*, December 5, 1976, 2, 98.

133 Crane: Stephen Crane, *The Red Badge of Courage* (1895; reprint, New York: Signet, 1960), 107.
"Flashbulb memories": *Cognition*, 5 (1977), 73–99.

134 Heath: *Dayton Daily News*, September 26, 1993.
Shaughnessy: Shaughnessy, *Walking on Alligators*, 195.
College freshman: Ken Macrorie, *Uptaught* (New York: Hayden, 1970), 23.

135 High school senior: Kimberly Denise Guthrie, *Dayton Daily News*, May 29, 1991.

137 Berryman: George Plimpton, ed., *Writers at Work*, 4th ser. (New York: Viking, 1976), 322.
Singer: Murray, *Shoptalk*, 87.
Updike: John Updike, *Assorted Prose* (New York: Knopf, 1965; New York: Fawcett, 1966), 177–78.
Cather, Silone: Meic Stephens, *A Dictionary of Literary Quotations* (London: Routledge, 1990), 173.
Dillard: Annie Dillard, *The Writing Life* (New York: Harper and Row, 1989), 44.
Dove: Rita Dove, *Through the Ivory Gate* (New York: Pantheon, 1992; New York: Vintage, 1993), 122.

139 Greene: Graham Greene, *Ways of Escape* (New York: Simon and Schuster, 1980), 161.

140 Cormier: Murray, *Shoptalk*, 72.

7. Should You Write in the Nude?

141 Carlyle: Donald Hall, ed., *The Oxford Book of American Literary Anecdotes* (New York: Oxford University Press, 1981), 223.
Cheever: *Newsweek*, March 14, 1977, 68.
Hugo, Riley: Robert Hendrickson, *The Literary Life and Other Curiosities* (New York: Viking, 1981), 6.

142 West: Donald M. Murray, *Shoptalk: Learning to Write with Writers* (Portsmouth, N.H.: Boynton/Cook, 1990), 65.
McPhee: Murray, *Shoptalk*, 58.

Maxwell: George Plimpton, ed., *Writers at Work*, 7th ser. (New York: Viking, 1986), 52–53.

Jordan: Murray, *Shoptalk*, 56.

Bernays: *Publishers Weekly*, September 16, 1983, 128.

Disraeli: Hendrickson, *Literary Life*, 4.

Keats: *The Independent*, November 16, 1990.

144   Graves: George Plimpton, ed., *Writers at Work*, 4th ser. (New York: Viking, 1976), 47–49.

Miller: Bernard Weisberger, ed., *The WPA Guide to America* (New York: Pantheon, 1985), 438.

Ibsen: Hendrickson, *Literary Life*, 4.

Schiller: Henry W. Nevinson, *Life of Friedrich Schiller* (London: Walter Scott, 1889), 188–89; *Psychology Today*, July 1975, 44.

Wiesel: George Plimpton, ed., *Writers at Work*, 8th ser. (New York: Viking, 1988), 235.

145   Hemingway, Woolf, Carroll, Grass: Hendrickson, *Literary Life*, 3; Murray, *Shoptalk*, 53.

Wolfe: Elizabeth Nowell, *Thomas Wolfe* (Garden City, N.Y.: Doubleday, 1960), 15.

Browning: *San Diego Union*, May 23, 1971.

Stevens: Brendan Gill, *Here at the New Yorker* (New York: Random House, 1975; New York: Berkeley, 1976), 61.

Twain, Capote, Welty, Wharton: Hendrickson, *Literary Life*, 3; George Plimpton, ed., *Writers at Work*, 1st ser. (New York: Viking, 1958), 294; *American Way*, December 1, 1993, 129; *New York Times*, November 10, 1976.

Styron, Gordon: *New York Times*, January 22, 1981.

146   Gass: George Plimpton, ed., *Writers at Work*, 5th ser. (New York: Viking, 1981), 271–72.

Mine-disposal experts: *New York Times Magazine*, January 23, 1994, 33.

Wideman: Murray, *Shoptalk*, 66.

Hemingway: Plimpton, *Writers at Work*, 1st ser., 103.

Allende: WYSO radio, Yellow Springs, Ohio, February 18, 1994.

Kerouac: Plimpton, *Writers at Work*, 4th ser., 382.

Walcott: Plimpton, *Writers at Work*, 8th ser. 272–73.

147 Barth, Tyler: Plimpton, *Writers at Work*, 7th ser., 236.

Graves: *New York Times*, November 22, 1981.

Neruda: Plimpton, *Writers at Work*, 5th ser., 59.

Bishop: George Plimpton, ed., *Writers at Work*, 6th ser. (New York: Viking, 1984), 129.

Rilke, Gass: Plimpton, *Writers at Work*, 5th ser., 259.

148 Williams, Eliot: Plimpton, *Writers at Work*, 6th ser., 129.

Ashbery: Plimpton, *Writers at Work*, 7th ser., 197.

One journalist: Greg Walter, *Philadelphia Daily News*, May 19, 1983.

Lyons: *Author's Guild Bulletin*, winter 1985, 9.

Rooney: *Tampa Tribune*, July 11, 1983.

150 Amis: Plimpton, *Writers at Work*, 5th ser., 192.

Jones: George Plimpton, ed., *Writers at Work*, 3d ser. (New York: Viking, 1967), 238.

O'Brien: Plimpton, *Writers at Work*, 7th ser., 261–62.

Kipling: Plimpton, *Writers at Work*, 1st ser., 17.

White: Plimpton, *Writers at Work*, 8th ser., 12; *Writer's Digest*, October 1978, 25.

152 Dillard: Annie Dillard, *The Writing Life* (New York: Harper and Row, 1989), 50.

Cather: Hendrickson, *Literary Life*, 3.

Doolittle: Hall, *American Literary Anecdotes*, 212–13.

McElroy: Tom LeClair and Larry McCaffery, ed., *Anything Can Happen: Interviews with Contemporary American Novelists* (Urbana, Ill.: University of Illinois Press, 1983), 236.

Dillard's friend: Dillard, *The Writing Life*, 15–16.

Moon: July 6, 1992, speech to Antioch Writer's Workshop; *Xenia Daily Gazette*, July 7, 1992.

153 Trillin: Murray, *Shoptalk*, 114.

O'Connor: Jon Winokur, *Writers on Writing* (Philadelphia: Running Press, 1987), 126.

Isherwood: Plimpton, *Writers at Work*, 4th ser., 239.

Chandler: George Plimpton, ed., *Writers at Work*, 2d ser. (New York: Viking, 1963), 248.

Godwin: *New York Times Book Review*, January 9, 1977, 31.
Allende: WYSO radio, February 18, 1994.

154 Wolfe: Tom Wolfe, *The Kandy-Kolored Tangerine-Flake Stream-line Baby* (New York: Farrar Straus Giroux, 1965; New York: Pocket, 1966), xii–xiv; *New York Times*, April 12, 1981.

Pascal: James Charlton, ed., *The Writer's Quotation Book* (Wainscott, N.Y.: Pushcart Press, 1991), 9.

155 Rorem: Joyce Carol Oates, ed., *First Person Singular: Writers on Their Craft* (Princeton, N.J.: Ontario Review Press, 1983), 100.

Ueland: Brenda Ueland, *If You Want to Write* (1938; reprint, St. Paul, Minn.: Schubert Club, 1984), 65.

156 Stendahl: *Shoptalk*, Murray, 63.

Mailer, Hemingway, Greene: Plimpton, *Writers at Work*, 3rd ser., 257; *San Diego Union*, May 23, 1971; Plimpton, *Writers at Work*, 7th ser., 228; Murray, *Shoptalk*, 54.

Hailey: Murray, *Shoptalk*, 54.

Trollope: Gerald Warner Brace, *The Stuff of Fiction* (New York: Norton, 1969), 24; Susan Shaughnessy, *Walking on Alligators: A Book of Meditations for Writers* (New York: Harper-Collins, 1993), 157.

157 Roth: Plimpton, *Writers at Work*, 7th ser., 271.
Maxwell: Plimpton, *Writers at Work*, 7th ser., 49.
Aiken: Plimpton, *Writers at Work*, 4th ser., 34.
Didion: *Ms.*, February 1977, 109.

158 Crichton: *Chicago Tribune*, January 27, 1994; *Los Angeles Times*, May 6, 1980; *American Way*, September 1975, 22; *New York*, April 16, 1973, 67; Michael Crichton, *Travels* (New York: Knopf, 1988), 347, 350.

Eliot: *Time*, October 31, 1977, 101.
Conrad: *The Economist*, March 14, 1981, 92.
Vonnegut: *New York Times*, April 12, 1981.
Cheever: *New York Times*, June 6, 1985.
Mailer: Plimpton, *Writers at Work*, 3rd ser., 259.
Wells: Winokur, *Writers on Writing*, 82.
Godwin: *New York Times Book Review*, January 9, 1977, 31.

159   White: Scott Elledge, *E. B. White: A Biography* (New York: Norton, 1984), 200–211; Dorothy Lobrano Guth, ed., *Letters of E. B. White* (New York: Harper and Row, 1976), 170.

        Porter: Joan Givner, *Katherine Anne Porter: A Life* (New York: Simon and Schuster, 1982), 475.

160   Malamud: Bill Gordon, *"How Many Books Do You Sell in Ohio?"* (Akron, Ohio: North Ridge Books, 1986), 105.

        dos Passos: Plimpton, *Writers at Work*, 4th ser., 84.

        Moravia: *San Diego Evening Tribune*, July 3, 1975.

        Trollope: Brace, *The Stuff of Fiction*, 24; James Sutherland, ed., *The Oxford Book of Literary Anecdotes* (Oxford: Clarendon Press, 1975), 246.

        Valéry: Plimpton, *Writers at Work*, 7th ser., 111.

        Faulkner: Glynne Robinson Betts, *Writers-in-Residence: American Authors at Home* (New York: Viking, 1981), 96.

161   Márquez: Plimpton, *Writers at Work*, 6th ser., 330.

        Burgess: Plimpton, *Writers at Work*, 4th ser., 326.

        Auel: Sybil Steinberg, ed., *Writing for Your Life* (Wainscott, N.Y.: Pushcart Press, 1992), 32.

        Lord: *Chicago Tribune*, June 30, 1990.

        Atwood: Oates, *First Person Singular*, 89.

162   Monet: *New York Times*, April 14, 1982.

163   Maxwell: Plimpton, *Writers at Work*, 7th ser., 54.

        Morrison: Claudia Tate, ed., *Black Women Writers at Work* (New York: Continuum, 1986), 130.

        Huxley: Plimpton, *Writers at Work*, 2d ser., 199.

8. A Little Help from Friends

165   Morrison: *The Nation*, October 24, 1981, 412.

        Ciardi: Janet Sternburg, *The Writer on Her Work*, vol. 2 (New York: Norton, 1991), 63.

        Kumin, Sexton: Sternburg, *The Writer on Her Work*, vol. 2, 63, 65–67; George Plimpton, ed., *Writers at Work*, 4th ser. (New York: Viking, 1976), 403; Diane Wood Middlebrook, *Anne Sexton: A Biography* (Boston: Houghton Mifflin, 1991), 79, 140–43.

167 Nabokov: Meic Stephens, *A Dictionary of Library Quotations* (London: Routledge, 1990), 83.

Swift: Michael Foot, introduction to *Gulliver's Travels* (1726; reprint, Middlesex, England: Penguin, 1967), 7.

Reed: *New York Times Book Review*, February 6, 1983, 24.

Larkin: George Plimpton, ed., *Writers at Work*, 7th ser. (New York: Viking, 1986), 154.

Weldon: Sybil Steinberg, ed., *Writing for Your Life* (Wainscott, N.Y.: Pushcart Press, 1992), 528.

Tyler: *New York Times Book Review*, February 6, 1983, 24.

Puzo: *Time*, August 28, 1978, 71.

Oates: *Philadelphia Inquirer*, September 21, 1982.

Gordimer: George Plimpton, ed., *Writers at Work*, 6th ser. (New York: Viking, 1984), 278.

Hoban: *Publishers Weekly*, May 15, 1981, 11.

168 Maxwell: Plimpton, *Writers at Work*, 7th ser., 64.

Turow: *All Things Considered*, National Public Radio, May 28, 1993.

Bellow: Plimpton, *Writers at Work*, 4th ser., 312; *Horizon*, April 1981, 53.

Allende: WYSO radio, Yellow Springs, Ohio, February 18, 1994.

Moore: George Plimpton, ed., *Writers at Work*, 2d ser. (New York: Viking, 1963), 74.

Harrison: Steinberg, *Writing for Your Life*, 240.

Stone: Charles Ruas, *Conversations with American Writers* (New York: Knopf, 1985), 284–85.

Turow: *All Things Considered*, May 28, 1993.

Steinbeck: *People*, July 9, 1990, 82.

Irving: *New York Times Book Review*, February 6, 1983, 11.

169 Tennyson: Plimpton, *Writers at Work*, 7th ser., 154.

Faulkner, Anderson: George Plimpton, ed., *Writers at Work*, 1st ser. (New York: Viking, 1958), 134–35.

170   Benchley's daughter-in-law: Clifton Fadiman, ed., *The Little, Brown Book of Anecdotes* (Boston: Little, Brown, 1985), 433.

Woolf, Wells: Frederic Spotts, ed., *Letters of Leonard Woolf* (San Diego: Harcourt Brace Jovanovich, 1989), 306–11.

172   Archer: *New York Times Book Review*, May 4, 1980, 46.

Adams: Donald Hall, ed., *The Oxford Book of American Literary Anecdotes* (New York: Oxford University Press, 1981), 122.

Lopate: Jon Winokur, *Writers on Writing* (Philadelphia: Running Press, 1987), 134.

174   White: *The Writer*, July 1966, 22–23.

175   Grumbach: Steinberg, *Writing for Your Life*, 227.

176   Eliot: James Charlton, ed., *The Writer's Quotation Book* (Wainscott, N.Y.: Pushcart Press, 1991), 120.

Gardner: *New York Times Book Review*, September 3, 1989, 16.

Faulkner: Plimpton, *Writers at Work*, 1st ser., 129; Stephen Oates, *William Faulkner* (New York: Harper and Row, 1987), 48–49.

Yates: *Horizon*, April 1981, 53.

177   Stamberg: Susan Stamberg, *Talk* (New York: Random House, 1993), 378.

Wolfe: Thomas Wolfe, *Of Time and the River* (New York: Scribner's, 1935).

Bellow, MacNeil: interview with MacNeil, WCAU radio, Philadelphia, March 17, 1989.

178   James, Claudel, Valéry: Plimpton, *Writers at Work*, 7th ser., 111.

Neruda: George Plimpton, ed., *Writers at Work*, 5th ser. (New York: Viking, 1981), 59.

Proust: Rosellen Brown, *Before and After* (New York: Farrar, Straus and Giroux, 1992), 94.

Caldwell: *Writer's Digest*, June 1974, 6.

Lewis: Fadiman, *Anecdotes*, 353.

179   Sexton: Plimpton, *Writers at Work*, 4th ser., 406.

Walters, *TV Guide*, March 21, 1981, 38.

180   Godwin: Janet Sternburg, *The Writer on Her Work*, vol. 1 (New York: Norton, 1980), 245–48.

White: Scott Elledge, *E. B. White: A Biography* (New York: Norton, 1984), 55–57; Beverly Gherman, *E. B. White: Some Writer!* (New York: Atheneum, 1992), 27.

Tan: Mickey Pearlman and Katherine Usher Henderson, ed., *Inter/View: Talks with America's Writing Women* (Lexington, Ky.: University Press of Kentucky, 1990), 15, 18–19; *New York Times*, March 19, 1989; *New York Times*, March 18, 1989; *Seattle Times*, January 10, 1991; *Chicago Tribune*, July 7, 1991; *People*, April 10, 1989, 150; Amy Tan, *The Joy Luck Club* (New York: Putnam, 1989), 5.

Morrison: *New York Times Book Review*, September 11, 1977, 48; *Washington Post*, September 30, 1977; *San Francisco Chronicle*, October 8, 1993.

181   Pound, Frost: Plimpton, *Writers at Work*, 2d ser., 14–15.

Hemingway: Carlos Baker, *Ernest Hemingway: A Life Story* (New York: Scribner's, 1969; New York: Bantam, 1970), 670.

Ozick: George Plimpton, ed., *Writers at Work*, 8th ser. (New York: Viking, 1988), 197–98.

182   Wakoski: Victoria Nelson, *On Writer's Block* (Boston: Houghton Mifflin, 1993), 58–59.

Updike: *New York Times Book Review*, August 16, 1981, 20.

Cerf, Lewis: Bennett Cerf, *At Random* (New York: Random House, 1977), 146–47.

183   Wodehouse: Plimpton, *Writers at Work*, 5th ser., 14–15.

184   Veteran of Iowa: Steinberg, *Writing for Your Life*, 112.

Friedman: Bonnie Friedman, *Writing Past Dark* (New York: HarperCollins, 1993), 57.

185   Sexton, Lowell: Plimpton, *Writers at Work*, 4th ser., 406.

9. The Courageous Writer

187   White: *The National Book Award: Writers on Their Craft and Their World* (New York: Book-of-the-Month, 1990), 52.

Ford: Ford Madox Ford, *It Was the Nightingale* (Philadelphia: Lippincott, 1933), 225.

188   Styron: George Plimpton, ed., *Writers at Work*, 1st ser. (New York: Viking, 1958), 18, 271–72.

Cheever: John Cheever, *The Journals of John Cheever* (New York: Knopf, 1991), 64.

Berry: Donald M. Murray, *Shoptalk: Learning to Write with Writers* (Portsmouth, N.H.: Boynton/Cook, 1990), 97.

Shaw: George Plimpton, ed., *Writers at Work*, 5th ser. (New York: Viking, 1981), 170.

189   Woolf: Joyce Carol Oates, *(Woman) Writer* (New York: Dutton, 1988), 5.

Zone, flow: *Los Angeles Times*, September 29, 1989; Mihalyi Csikszentmihalyi, *Flow: The Psychology of Optimal Experience* (New York: HarperCollins, 1991).

190   Allende: *New York Times*, February 4, 1988; WYSO radio, Yellow Springs, Ohio, February 18, 1994; WYSO, September 2, 1994.

Bowen: *Atlantic Monthly*, December 1957, 87.

191   Merrill: George Plimpton, ed., *Writers at Work*, 6th ser. (New York: Viking, 1984), 311.

192   Sexton: Plimpton, *Writers at Work*, 4th ser., 402.

193   Cowley: Plimpton, *Writers at Work*, 1st ser. 19.

Faulkner: Plimpton, *Writers at Work*, 1st ser., 125.

Anderson: Clifton Fadiman, ed., *The Little, Brown Book of Anecdotes* (Boston: Little, Brown, 1985), 17.

194   Burgess: George Plimpton, ed., *Writers at Work*, 4th ser. (New York: Viking, 1976), 344.

Didion: Plimpton, *Writers at Work*, 5th ser., 357.

196   Brontës: Rebecca Fraser, *The Brontës* (New York: Crown, 1988), 57, 90–91, 267, 312–15; Daphne du Maurier, *The Infernal World of Branwell Brontë* (Garden City, N.Y.: Doubleday, 1966), 221, 239–43, 275, 287, 289; Victoria Nelson, *On Writer's Block*, (Boston: Houghton Mifflin, 1993), 80–81.

Berryman: Plimpton, *Writers at Work*, 4th ser., 322.

McGuane: *Writer's Yearbook*, 1977, 10–11.

197   Snodgrass, Sexton: Diane Wood Middlebrook, *Anne Sexton: A Biography* (Boston: Houghton Mifflin, 1991), 52, 81.

Steinem: *Writer's Digest*, February 1974, 14.

198 Vonnegut: *Philadelphia Inquirer*, June 26, 1976.

Mailer: George Plimpton, ed., *Writers at Work*, 3d series (New York: Viking, 1967), 255.

200 Block: Lawrence Block, *Write for Your Life* (Fort Myers, Fla.: Lawrence Block, 1986), 44.

202 Cather: Glynne Robinson Betts, *Writers-in-Residence: American Authors at Home* (New York: Viking, 1981), 124.

White: Dorothy Lobrano Guth, ed., *Letters of E. B. White* (New York: Harper and Row, 1976), 417.

203 Dove: *Bill Moyers' Journal*, PBS Television, April 4, 1994.

Selected Bibliography

Auden, W. H. *A Certain World.* New York: Viking, 1970.

Betts, Glynne Robinson. *Writers-in-Residence: American Authors at Home.* New York: Viking, 1981.

Cerf, Bennett. *At Random.* New York: Random House, 1977.

Charlton, James, ed. *The Writer's Quotation Book.* Wainscott, N.Y.: Pushcart Press, 1991.

Cheever, John. *The Journals of John Cheever.* New York: Knopf, 1991.

Delbanco, Nicholas, and Laurence Goldstein, ed. *Writers and Their Craft: Short Stories and Essays on the Narrative.* Detroit: Wayne State University Press, 1991.

Dillard, Annie. *The Writing Life.* New York: Harper and Row, 1989.

Elledge, Scott. *E. B. White: A Biography.* New York: Norton, 1984.

Fadiman, Clifton, ed. *The Little, Brown Book of Anecdotes.* Boston: Little, Brown, 1985.

Friedman, Bonnie. *Writing Past Dark.* New York: HarperCollins, 1993.

Gordon, Bill. *"How Many Books Do You Sell in Ohio?"* Akron, Ohio: North Ridge Books, 1986.

Guth, Dorothy Lobrano, ed. *Letters of E. B. White.* New York: Harper and Row, 1976.

Hall, Donald, ed. *The Oxford Book of American Literary Anecdotes.* New York: Oxford University Press, 1981.

Hendrickson, Robert. *The Literary Life and Other Curiosities.* New York: Viking, 1981.

LeClair, Tom, and Larry McCaffery, ed. *Anything Can Happen: Interviews with Contemporary American Novelists* Urbana, Ill.: University of Illinois Press, 1983.

Murray, Donald M. *Shoptalk: Learning to Write with Writers.* Portsmouth, N.H.: Boynton/Cook, 1990.

Nelson, Victoria. *On Writer's Block.* Boston: Houghton Mifflin, 1993.

Oates, Joyce Carol, ed. *First Person Singular: Writers on Their Craft.* Princeton, N.J.: Ontario Review Press, 1983.

Parsons, Nicholas, ed. *The Book of Literary Lists.* New York: Facts on File, 1987.

Pearlman, Mickey, and Katherine Usher Henderson, ed. *Inter/View: Talks with America's Writing Women.* Lexington, Ky.: University Press of Kentucky, 1990.

Plimpton, George, ed. *Writers at Work.* 1st ser. New York: Viking, 1958.

———. *Writers at Work.* 2d ser. New York: Viking, 1963.

———. *Writers at Work.* 3d ser. New York: Viking, 1967.

———. *Writers at Work.* 4th ser. New York: Viking, 1976.

———. *Writers at Work.* 5th ser. New York: Viking, 1981.

———. *Writers at Work.* 6th ser. New York: Viking, 1984.

———. *Writers at Work.* 7th ser. New York: Viking, 1986.

———. *Writers at Work.* 8th ser. New York: Viking, 1988.

Rood, Karen L., ed. *American Literary Almanac.* New York: Facts on File, 1988.

Ruas, Charles. *Conversations with American Writers.* New York: Knopf, 1985.

Shaughnessy, Susan. *Walking on Alligators: A Book of Meditations for Writers.* New York: HarperCollins, 1993.

Steinberg, Sybil, ed. *Writing for Your Life.* Wainscott, N.Y.: Pushcart Press, 1992.

Stephens, Meic. *A Dictionary of Literary Quotations.* London: Routledge, 1990.

Sternburg, Janet. *The Writer on Her Work.* Vol. 1. New York: Norton, 1980.

———. *The Writer on Her Work.* Vol. 2. New York: Norton, 1991.

Sutherland, James, ed. *The Oxford Book of Literary Anecdotes.* Oxford: Clarendon Press, 1975.

Tate, Claudia, ed. *Black Women Writers at Work.* New York: Continuum, 1986.

Ueland, Brenda. *If You Want to Write.* 1938. Reprint, St. Paul, Minn.: Schubert Club, 1984.

Winokur, Jon. *Writers on Writing.* Philadelphia: Running Press, 1987.